幼保 英語検定

Level Pre- **1級** テキスト

【著者】 一般社団法人 幼児教育・保育英語検定協会

BOOKFORE
ブックフォレ 株式会社ブックフォレ

目次

目次

目次

目次

 ＊テキスト音源は、こちらのホームページよりダウンロードをしてください。

HP https://bookfore.co.jp/glh/download/

幼児教育・保育英語検定協会
（略称：幼保英語検定協会）

幼児教育、保育環境の国際的なグローバル化に対応できる幼稚園教諭及び保育士等幼児教育者養成の一環として、全国の幼稚園・保育園並びに幼稚園教諭・保育士養成学科を有する大学・短大及び専門学校と連携・協力して、幼保英語検定の実施を通し必要な実用的な英語の習得及び向上に資するため、英語の能力を判定し、またさまざまな活躍の機会を拡げその能力を養成することにより、日本の幼児教育、保育現場の向上に寄与することを目的としています。

また、諸外国における乳幼児教育分野の研究成果等を日本に紹介し、乳幼児教育分野の発展に寄与する活動にも積極的に取り組むことを目的とします。

幼児教育・保育英語検定
（略称：幼保英語検定）

特色

幼保英語検定は、幼稚園、こども園及び保育園等幼児教育施設において、英語でのコミュニケーション力の習得状況を知り、さらに向上させる機会となります。乳幼児との会話、園内の教育・保育に焦点をあて、現場に即した実用的な英語を習得できることが大きな特色です。

園内教育・保育及び保護者との日常会話から連絡・交流に必要な題材まで、受検者の学習を考慮し工夫した内容になっており、楽しみながら知識を深められる構成となっています。「入門レベル」から責任者として活躍できる「専門レベル」までの5段階で構成されており、英語力の向上が実感できます。資格を取得すると、幼児教育、保育分野で幅広く活用することができ、幼児教育、保育環境の国際的なグローバル化に対応できる実用的な英語を取得できます。

About Youho Eigo Kentei

Youho Eigo Kentei (Test of English for Early Childhood Educators) is designed for early childhood educators based on the daily routines and annual curriculum of Japanese preschools and kindergartens. This test is administered by Youho Eigo Kentei Kyokai (Organization of English for Early Childhood Educators). The test gives test takers a guideline to increase their language and comprehension levels, of both Japanese and English, by focusing on early childhood education, assessing reading, writing, listening, and speaking skills. We work closely with over 200 universities, colleges, technical schools, and high schools in Japan that have early childhood education departments. We also work with universities and Japanese schools overseas for non-native Japanese speakers who want to improve their professional skills. The test certificate shows that the person designated possesses the English proficiency level of the grade in which he or she has been certified.

本書について

本書は、幼保英語検定準1級のテキストです。
本書は、「登園の楽しみ」から「就学前の教育」までの7つ章で、各章とも、保護者・園児との会話、各種文章作成と参考資料から構成されています。

会話文は、先生と保護者との会話、先生と園児との会話から成り立っており、各会話は、左のページに日本語による会話を記載し、右のページに英訳を記載しています。
本書は、幼保英語検定準1級の能力目安に準拠し、園児や保護者と幼保英語をつかって円滑なコミュニケーションを行うことができ、園で必要な文書の作成に支障がないレベルの英語力の習得を目的としています。
幼保英語検定準1級の目安は、大学中級程度です。
本書の特色
日本における保育、幼児教育現場に即した内容を前提としています。
園での日常活動で使われる英語や英語表現を身につけることができるよう工夫しており、紹介シーンも、日本の習慣や行事など、日本での保育、幼児教育を前提としています。

① 説明や解説の文章の中に記載している英語の表記には、「　」（カギカッコ）をつけています。「　」（カギカッコ）は日本語の文章の会話文を表記する方法として使われ、文中の英語には通常、""（クォーテーション）や斜体で区別しますが、「　」（カギカッコ）は区別が明確にしやすいため、本書では説明や解説の際に日本語及び英語のイディオムや単語の区分方法として採用しています。

② 人物の呼称は、英語圏では園児はファーストネームを使い、先生や保護者などにはMr.、Mrs.、Ms.をつけて使いますが、日本の生活慣習から違和感を生じないよう、英会話文でも、園児は「○○-kun、○○-chan」、先生は「○○-sensei」、保護者には「○○-san」と表現しています。

③ 会話文は日本文が一文でも、英文は2文に、またその逆になっている文もありますが、これは日本語、英語それぞれが自然な会話になるように作成したことによります。

本書を十分に学習され、早期に幼保英語検定準1級に合格されることをお祈りしております。

本書では、実際の園の会話を想定できるよう、バーチャルプリスクールを設定しています。

園名　　　　フォレガーデン園

所在地	東京都港区麻布2丁目
最寄駅	北東線麻布駅徒歩10分
避難場所	有栖川山公園(通称アリス公園)
電話	03－987－9876　　　メール　azabu2@ac.ko.jp

園の紹介　　0歳児より未就学児まで

乳児1歳児未満	10名
2歳児未満	15名
2歳児	15名
3歳児	20名
4歳児	20名
5歳児各	30名

園の内容　　2階建て、保健室、園庭、プール、調理室、屋上広場あり

主な登場人物

園長	山田	けいこ
(園長代行)	ポール	山田
事務長	青山	えりか
保育士	鈴木	よしこ
職員	木村	ゆか
新米先生	南田	まどか
園児	荒木	たえこ　　保護者
園児	小野	ひろし　　保護者

第1章　登園の楽しみ

Chapter 1　　Going to School

園児は乗り物が大好きですから、バス通園は大人気です。しかし、交通ルールを守らないととても危険です。初めてバス通園をする園児に交通ルールを英語で説明しましょう。登園時に雪が降っていると、危険を伴うこともありますが、雪の日の楽しみもあります。園児と英語で会話してみましょう。

シーン1	園バスによる通園	Scene 1	Taking the School Bus
シーン2	雪の日の登園	Scene 2	A Snowy Day

園バスによる通園

たえこの通園バスの申し込みをしたいのですが。

わかりました。では、まず通園バスの利用方法をご説明します。

通園バスは2コースあります。

たえちゃんの場合は、カモメバスのコースだと思います。

カモメバスのコーススケジュール表はこちらです。

ありがとうございます。えーと、3丁目郵便局前が一番近いバス停みたいですね。

そうですね。このバス停だと、たえちゃんを朝7時半頃お迎えに行き、帰りの時間は午後3時頃になります。

このバス停を利用している園児は現在2人いますので、もしたえちゃんが申し込んだら、全部で3人がこのバス停を利用することになります。

こちらが通園バスの利用料金や支払い方法の詳細です。お申し込みの前によく読んでください。

わかりました。ありがとうございます。

Vocabulary

申し込む sign up	**コース** route
一番近い closest 合	**およそ** around＋数詞
計〜 a total of 〜	

Taking the School Bus

I would like to sign Tae up for the school bus.

Okay. Then let me first tell you about our bus service.

The Fore Garden Preschool bus currently runs along 2 routes.

I think Tae-chan will be on bus that runs along the Kamome route.

Here's the Kamome bus schedule.

Thank you. Let's see. Our closest bus station looks like it is in front of the 3-chome post office.

Yes. If this is your bus stop, then the bus will pick Tae-chan up at around 7:30 am and drop her off at around 3:00 pm.

We currently have two other children using this bus stop, so there'll be a total of three children on that bus after Tae-chan signs up.

Here are all the details about the bus fee and the method of payment. Please read them carefully before you sign up.

Okay. Thank you.

Point 1

close

形容詞で「接近した、親密な」という意味を表し、活用は closer, closest となります。

園バスによる通園

たえちゃん、おはよう！

園に行く準備はいいかな？さぁ、バスに乗ってください。

バスに乗ったら、席に座って、必ずシートベルトをしてね、いいかな？

そろそろ出発しますよ。

はーい、シートベルトしました。

はい、いいですね。では、出発しましょう。

次のバス停ではもっとたくさんのお友達がバスを待っていますよ。

たえちゃん、バスに乗るのは慣れてる？

うん、だいじょうぶ。いつもママとバスに乗っているから。

それはよかった。園までは約15分ですから、しっかりと前の手すりをにぎっててね、いいかな？

Vocabulary

〜を締める　buckle 〜

すぐに〜する　be about to 〜

バスに乗る　go on the bus

（交通手段として、go by 〜を用いる場合は無冠詞です。（例）go by bus）

Picking Up the Children

Good morning, Tae-chan!

Are you ready to go to school? Okay, let's get on the bus.

Sit down after you get on the bus and make sure you buckle your seat belt, okay?

We're about to leave.

Okay, I buckled my seat belt.

Okay, good. Now, let's go.

There are more students waiting for the bus at the next stop.

Tae-chan, are you comfortable with taking the bus?

Yes, I'm okay. I always go on the bus with my mommy.

That's good to hear. It'll take about 15 minutes to get to the school, so hold on to the handle tightly, okay?

Point 1

乗り物(車など)に乗る/降りる get in/get out

(バス・電車・飛行機など)に乗る/降りる get on/get off

in/out は四方を囲まれていることが意識できるような空間に使います。乗用車は天井や窓に手が届くので、乗り降りを言うときは get in/get out を使います。一方、バスや電車などは、乗用車に比べて空間が広く、床に立つイメージなので、get on/get off と言います。

幼稚園通園バス利用申込書 （要約）

年　月　日

フォレガーデン園
園長　山田　けいこ　殿

申込者（保護者）氏名　　　　　　　印

下記誓約事項を順守することを確約の上、幼稚園通園バスを利用したいので、下記のとおり申し込みます。

記

（フリガナ）	
園児氏名	性別　男・女
生年月日	年　月　日（　歳　ヵ月）※4月1日時点
住　　所	
電　　話	緊急連絡先
乗降希望場所	

1. 登園、降園とも利用　　2. 登園のみ利用　　3. 降園のみ利用

通園バス利用誓約事項

通園バスの利用にあたって、子どもの安全確保に努め、また子どもにきちんと説明することを誓います。

　　1　所定の場所まで責任ある大人が送迎します。

　　2　バスを待っている時は子どもの安全を確保します。

　　3　バスから降りたら、責任ある大人が安全を十分に確保します。

　　4　常に交通ルールを守り、子どもの模範となります。

ABC

Let's Try ①

Sign-up Sheet for Students Riding the Fore Garden Preschool Bus

Date: / /	
Principal Keiko Yamada	
Applicant's Name:	
I understand the contents of this sign-up sheet and have provided the appropriate information required to apply for a seat on the bus.	
Student's Name Gender Boy/ Girl	
Birthdates / / (Yrs. Months) ∗ (by 4/1 Entrance Date)	
Address	
Telephone No. Emergency Contact No.	
Location for pick-up:	
1.Require both pick up and drop-off 2.Only pick-up 3.Only drop-off	

The Conditions for Using Fore Garden School Bus

I promise to uphold the passenger safety conditions listed below and explain them to my child

1. A designated caregiver will both accompany the child to the bus stop and pick the child up.
2. While waiting for the bus the caregiver will ensure the child's safety.
3. The caregiver will ensure the child's safety after getting off the bus.
4. I will follow these rules and be a positive role model to my child with regard to traffic rules.

つくってみましょう ② おたより編

春と秋の交通安全週間

園児に守ってもらいたい交通安全ルールを作成しましょう（要約）

歩く時の約束

1. 道路を渡るときは横断歩道や歩道橋を渡りましょう。

2. 信号が赤の時は止まりましょう。信号が青に変わったことを確認したら、右を見て、左を見て、もう一度右を見てから、車が来ていないことを確かめて渡りま しょう。

3. 道路を渡っているときも車が来ていないかなど周りの状況を確かめましょう。

4. 道路に駐車している車のそばでは、絶対に遊ばないようにしましょう。

5. 道路には飛び出さないようにしましょう。

自転車に乗る時の約束

1. ヘルメットをかぶりましょう。

2. 友だちとならんで走ることはやめましょう。一列になって走りましょう。

3. まわりが暗くなったら、必ずライトをつけましょう。

4. 信号を守りましょう。

5. 13歳以下の子どもは自転車に乗る際に歩道を走りましょう。

6. 歩行者が多いときは、自転車からおりて押して歩きましょう。

自動車に乗るときの約束

1. 6歳以下の子どもは必ず体に合ったチャイルドシートを使用しましょう。

2. チャイルドシートは車の後部席に設置するのが一番安全です。車にチャイルドシートが安全に正しく設置されているか気をつけましょう。

Let's Try ②

Traffic Safety Tips

Safety Points to Remember:

When Walking on the Street

1. Use pedestrian underpasses or pedestrian bridges.

2. Stop at red lights. Before crossing, make sure that a car is not coming, check both directions — to your right, then left, then right again—and only then begin to cross.

3. Even when crossing, pay attention to the flow of traffic, and always take notice of the situation around you.

4. Never play near parked vehicles on the road.

5. Never run out into the road.

When Riding a Bicycle

1. Wear a helmet.

2. Do not ride your bicycle side-by-side with a friend. Always ride in a line.

3. Make sure to turn your bicycle light on when it gets dark.

4. Obey traffic lights.

5. Children under 13 must use pedestrians walkways when riding a bicycle.

6. Get off your bicycle and walk it if there is a risk of obstructing pedestrian traffic.

When Riding a Car

1. Children under 6 must use a child seat of appropriate size.

2. It is safest to put the car seat in the back seat of the car. Be sure that the child seat is securely and properly fastened.

つくってみましょう ③ おたより編

保護者の方に、交通安全の呼びかけを しましょう（要約）

保護者各位

フォレガーデン園
園長　山田　けいこ

交通安全週間が始まりました。警察より交通安全の呼びかけがありましたので保護者の皆様にお知らせ致します。くれぐれもお子様の安全に気を配り、お子様の模範となるよう、園からもお願い致します。

子どもは保護者の後を追います。常にお子様が保護者から離れないよう、目を離さないでください。多くの事故は保護者と一緒に道路を渡ろうとして発生しています。保護者の後を追いかけて車にひかれて亡くなったといういたましい交通事故もたびたび発生しています。

特に、お買い物の途中、園バスの乗降時などは、お子様から目を離さないでください。

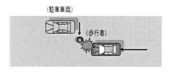

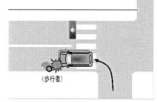

Let's Try ③

Traffic Safety Letter to Parents

Dear Parents,

Traffic Safety Week has started. The local police department has informed us of the traffic safety rules that they would like us to pass on to the parents of our school. We appreciate your cooperation to make sure your child knows and follows these safety rules. Please be a good role model for your child, as well.

Children will often run after their parents, so please take care to keep your child close at all times!

Many accidents happen when children are crossing the street with their parents. Too often parents walk ahead and children run after them, which has been the cause of fatal accidents.

Please keep an eye on your children at all times, especially while shopping, during pick-up and drop-off times at the school bus stops.

Sincerely,
Principal
Keiko Yamada

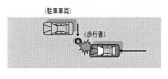

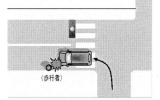

雪の日の登園

おはようございます。なんて日なんでしょう！昨晩はすごい吹雪でしたね！

おはようございます。ええ、昨晩からの大雪で歩道が滑るので、登園は大丈夫かと心配していました。

そうですね。こんなに雪が積もるとは思っていませんでした。私たちも早めに登園して、園への通路の雪かきをしたんですよ。

それは、大変でしたね！

道路は渋滞していて、車もバスもとてもゆっくり走っていました。そのせいでここに来るのに時間がかかりました。

子どもたちは大喜びですけどね！

今日は、みんなで雪だるまを作るつもりです。楽しくなりそうです！

それはそうですよね、子どもたちは、雪合戦も楽しみにしてるんじゃないですか？

ええ、そうだと思います。

Vocabulary

猛吹雪　blizzard

～を心配する　be concerned about ～

交通渋滞　bumper-to-bumper

雪合戦　snowball fight

吹雪　snowstorm

滑りやすい　slippery

雪かきをする　shovel snow

A Snowy Day

Good morning. What a day! It was quite a blizzard last night!

Good morning. Yes, I was very concerned about getting in to school because the roads were all slippery from the heavy snow last night.

Yes. We were not expecting so much snow. We came in early and shoveled the snow on the walkway to clear a path up to the school.

That must have been hard work!

The traffic was bumper-to-bumper and the cars and buses were running very slowly. It took a long time to get here.

The children are so excited and happy by the snow, though!

We are going to make snowmen today. It's going to be so much fun!

Yes, I'm sure, and I guess they are probably looking forward to having a snow ball fight too, aren't they?

Yes, I'm sure they are.

Point 1

What a day!　なんて日なんでしょう！

We were not expecting 〜　〜とは予想していなかった

雪の日の登園

今日は、雪がたくさん降りましたね。

みんな、園に来る途中でころびませんでしたか？

何回もころびそうになりました！道路がすごくツルツルだったよ！

まぁ、でも無事に園に来られてよかったわ。たくさん雪が降ったから、今日は、予定を変更して、園庭で雪だるまを作ろうか？

やったー！

いままでに、雪だるまを作ったことある人いるかな？

ぼくあるよ。

そう、じゃあ、雪だるまをどうやってつくるか知ってるわね。お外に出る前に雪だるまの作り方を教えるね。雪だるまは、最初に雪のお団子を作って、それを雪の中で転がして大きくしていきます。

二つの大きな雪の玉を作って、重ねます。

あまり大きくしないでね、抱えられなくなりますから。

二つの大きな雪の玉で雪だるまの体ができあがったら、この炭で目と口をつくります。最後に枝でお鼻をつくってね。

では、みんな手袋とコートを着て、お外にでる準備をしてください！

A Snowy Day

It snowed a lot today.

Did anyone fall down on their way to school?

I almost slipped many times! The streets were so slippery!

Well, it is good that you made it to school safely. Since there is so much snow, let's change our plan for today and why don't we make a snowman in the playground?

Yeah!

Have any of you made a snowman before?

I made one before.

Good, then you know how to make it. Before we go out, let me tell you how to make a snowman. First, make a ball of snow, then roll it around in the snow to make it bigger.

You need to make two big balls of snow and put one on top of the other.

Don't make your balls of snow too big, otherwise we won't be able to carry them.

After you are done making the body of the snowman with the two big balls of snow, we will make the eyes and a mouth using this charcoal. Finally, we'll make the nose with a branch.

Okay, get your gloves and coats on, and let's get ready to go outside!

Point 1

Snowman について

日本の雪だるまは２つの雪玉で作りますが、英語圏では３つ重ねて作ります。日本では「雪だるま」と言う名の通り、座禅を組んでいるだるまの形を模しているのに対し、３段の雪だるまは、上から頭、胴、足を表していて、立っている姿をしています。

単語と英語の表現 ①

雪の日に関する表現

1. 今日はとても冷え込んでいて、吐く息も白くなります。

2. 雪が降っています。たくさん積もりそうですね。
   - 地面の雪を見てください。
   - 積もってきていますよ。

3. 雪が吹雪いています。

4. みぞれが降ってきました。

5. そのままにしておくことで園児が転ぶと危ないので、スコップで、玄関の雪かきをしましょう。

6. 屋根の雪下ろしをしないと、重さで屋根が壊れてしまうかもしれません。

7. 今朝の寒さで、水たまりに氷が張っています。

8. 軒にできた氷柱が、温かい天気でとけだしました。

9. 手袋をしているのに、寒さで指がかじかんでいます。

10. 雪をはたいてから部屋に入ります。

11. あまりの寒さで、水道管が凍って水が出ません。

ABC

Important Words and Phrases ①

Useful Phrases for a Snowy Day

1. It's so chilly that I can see my breath today.

2. It's snowing. It looks like it is going to accumulate quite a bit.
   - Look at all the snow on the ground.
   - It's really sticking.

3. It's a blizzard.

4. A mixture of snow and rain is falling.

5. Let's shovel the snow at the entrance way, because children might slip if leave it as it is.

6. If we don't shovel the snow off of the roof, the building may collapse.

7. Ice has formed on the puddle from the freezing temperatures this morning.

8. The icicles along the roof have started melting from the warm weather.

9. Although we have our gloves on, our fingers are numb with cold.

10. Brush the snow off your clothes before going inside.

11. There is no running water coming out because the water pipe has frozen from the cold weather.

BC

単語と英語の表現 ②

天気に関する単語と表現
Terms Used for Weather

氷点下	below zero	天気図	weather map
凍雨	ice pellets/sleet	天気予報	weather forecast
にわか雪	snow shower	降水確率	chance of rain/snow
雹（ひょう）	hail	花粉情報	pollen report
霰（あられ）	snow pellets	桜前線	cherry blossom front
吹雪	blizzard	注意報	warning
みぞれ	mixture of snow	湿度	humidity
風向き	wind direction	落雷	lightning
熱帯低気圧	tropical low	集中豪雨	local severe rain
暴風雨	rainstorm	熱帯夜	humid hot night
洪水	flood	猛暑	excessive hot weather
おおむね晴れ	mostly sunny	快晴	clear sky
一時小雪が舞う	occasional light snow		
もやがかかる	misty	断続的に雨	continuous rain

Weather Map（要約）

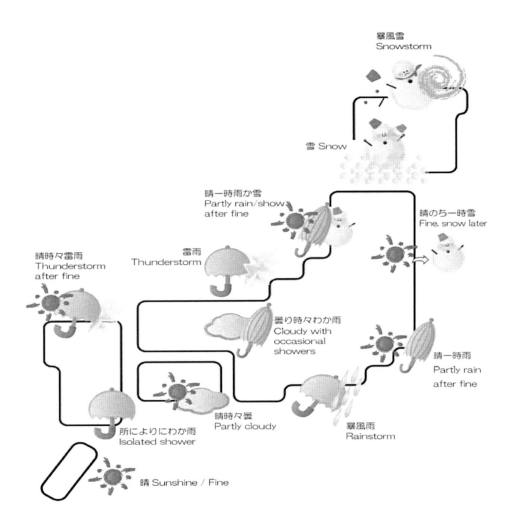

暴風雪
Snowstorm

雪 Snow

晴一時雨か雪
Partly rain/show
after fine

晴のち一時雪
Fine, snow later

晴時々雷雨
Thunderstorm
after fine

雷雨
Thunderstorm

曇り時々わか雨
Cloudy with
occasional
showers

晴一時雨
Partly rain
after fine

所によりにわか雨
Isolated shower

晴時々曇
Partly cloudy

暴風雨
Rainstorm

晴 Sunshine / Fine

「I'm ready」と「I'm all ready」

お出かけの時「Are you ready?（準備できた？）」への返事は、「Yes, I'm ready!（はい、準備できました！）」です。これに「all」を加えて「I'm all ready!」と表現すると、「完璧！準備万端よ！」の意味に変わります。

「Do what you want to.」と「Do what you want!」

「to」が入るか入らないかで意味が変わります。

「Do what you want to.」は、「好きなようにやってごらんなさい。」という意味です。「to」をぬいて、「Do what you want.」と表現すると、「勝手にしなさい。」という意味に変わります。

「Hiroshi-kuns being difficult.」と「Hiroshi-kun's difficult.」

同じ「difficult」でも「being」が入るかどうかで意味が変わります。

ひろし君がだだをこねているときに先生が「ひろし君がだだをこねて、困っちゃうわ。」と言う時「being」をいれて「Hiroshi-kun's being difficult.」と表現します。「Hiroshi-kun's difficult.」は、「ひろし君は、気難しくて対応しにくい、やりにくいな。」となります。

「is being」（現在進行形）はその時のみの状況を指し、「is」（現在形）は日常の状況や性質を表します。

「Do you understand?」と「Do you understand me?」

「Do you understand?」は、「わかる〜？」と優しく尋ねる場合に使います。

「me」を入れて「Do you understand me?」となると、「ちょっと、わかったの？」に変わります。

なかなかいうことを聞かない子どもに「ママの言っていることがきちんとわかっているの？」と言うときにはこちらを使います。「me」を入れると少し表現が強く感じられます。

第２章　楽しい園の行事 ①
（夏から秋）

Chapter 2　　Fun School Events ①
（Summer ～ Fall）

楽しい行事の会話を練習しましょう

> 園園には、1年を通じて様々な楽しい行事がいっぱいあります。各行事は、保護者に園児の成長を見て頂く大事な機会です。また、保護者とのコミュニケーションを図るよい機会でもあります。この章では夏から秋までの行事を取り上げています。2級テキストの「こどもの日」「遠足」での会話とあわせて、表現を学習しましょう。

七夕まつり

👨 まあ、今日は、短冊作ったのですね。

👩 はい、今日はみんなで七夕の工作をやったんですよ。

👨 もうそんな時期だったかしら？そうでしたね、あさってが七夕ですね。天気が良いといいけど。

👩 そうですね、子どもたちも、天の川を見るのを楽しみにしてるんですよ。

👨 ええ。でも、町の明かりが明るいせいで天気が良くても見つけるのは大変ですから、天の川は見れないかもしれないですね。

👩 そうですね。子どもたちは星をはっきり見ることができなくてかわいそうですね。

👨 ひろしは短冊に何を書いたのかしら。まあ！大きくなったら、サッカー選手になれますようにと書いてあるわ。

👩 ええ、ひろし君に、大きくなったら何になりたいか書いてね、何でもいいのよと言ったんです。すぐにそれを書いてましたよ。

👨 ひろし、がんばってね。夢がかなうといいね。

Vocabulary

短冊 streamer

天の川 Milky Way

大きくなる（成長する） grow up

実現する come true

Tanabata Festival

Oh, you made streamers today.

Yes, we did an art activity for Tanabata today.

Is it that time of the year already? That's right, Tanabata is the day after tomorrow. I hope the weather will be fine.

Yes, the kids are looking forward to seeing the Milky Way too.

I know. The children may not be able to see it though because the city lights are so bright, making it hard to find, even when the weather is fine.

Yes, you're right. It's a pity that kids can't see the stars clearly in the sky.

Let me see what Hiroshi wrote on his streamer. Wow! He wrote that he wants to be a soccer player when he grows up.

Yes, I told him to write anything he wants to be when he grows up. He wrote that right away.

Good luck, Hiroshi. I hope your dream comes true.

Point 1　though　（〜だが）

though は本来従属接続詞で、後ろに主語述語を伴って主節に対して逆接の内容を表します。しかし会話では、主節の内容がすでに述べられていたり明確で言う必要がないときは主節を省略し、本来後ろに続く主語述語を前に出して、「〜だけどね」と言う表現として使います。本文の" The children may not be able to see it though …"は、"the kids are looking forward to seeing the Milky Way too"を主節として、「子供達はそれ（天の川）が見えないかも知れませんけどね」の意味になります。

Point 2　七夕まつりを説明してみましょう　Tanabata Festival

7月7日に、短冊に願いごとなどを書き、笹に飾りつけて、夢が叶うように星にお願いをします。

Tanabata Festival, which takes place on July 7th, is celebrated by writing down a wish on a streamer, tying it to a bamboo branch, and praying to the stars to make the wish come true.

七夕まつり

7月7日は何の日か知っていますか？

七夕です！

そうですね。七夕の日ですね。七夕は、年に一回、7月7日におり姫とひこ星が天の川で会える大切な日なのですよ。

お願い事を色とりどりの短冊に書いてそれを笹につるして願い事が叶うようにお祈りします。

では、みんなに色のついた短冊を配りますから、短冊の後ろにクレヨンで自分のお願いを書いてね。

何を書こうかな？

そうね、将来についてお願いしたいことだったら何でも書いていいのよ。もっと速く走れるようになりたいとか、ピアノが上手になりたいとか、背が高くなりたいとか。自分が書きたいことなんでもいいのよ。

サッカー選手になりたい！

いいじゃない！そう書いたらいいわ。

今日は笹をみんなの分準備してあります。短冊にお願い事を書いたら短冊を笹に吊るせるように糸をつけてね。

この糸を「こより」と言うのよ。それで、終わったら飾ったものをおうちに持って帰ってくださいね！

笹をおうちに持って帰ったら、おうちの人にも短冊にお願い事を書いてもらって同じようにつるしてね。

Vocabulary

～にとって (～において) 特別です be special about ～

～の願いが叶うように祈る Pray for one's wishes to come true

配る pass out

Tanabata Festival

 Do you know what is special about July 7th?

It's Tanabata!

Yes. It's Tanabata. The seventh day of July is an important day because Orihime and Hikoboshi are allowed to meet in the Milky Way. This can happen only once a year.

People write their wishes on colorful narrow strips of paper, hang them on bamboo branches, and pray for their wishes to come true.

Now, I will pass out a strip of colored paper, so write your wish on the back of it with crayons.

What should I write?

Well, you can write anything that you wish for in the future, like to run faster, play piano better, or grow taller. You can write anything you want.

I want to be a good soccer player!

Great! Then, that is what you should write.

I have bamboo branches for everyone today. Once you have written your wishes on your strip of paper, you need to attach a string to it so you can hang it from the bamboo branch.

We call this string, koyori. Now, when you're finished, you can take your decorations home!

After you take your bamboo branch home, you can ask your family members to write their wishes down and hang them from it.

Point 1

You can write anything（that）you want.

関係代名詞「that」の省略：目的格の関係代名詞は制限用法の場合省略され、特に口語調のときはその傾向が強いようです。

クレヨンの持ち方を教えます

あら、ひろし君、そのクレヨンの持ち方だと、字が書きづらいだけでなく、線をまっすぐ引いたり、塗ったりするのも難しいわね。

みんな、短冊に願い事を書くのをやめて、先生のほうを見てください。

クレヨンでも、絵の具の筆でも、マジックでも持ち方は同じですよ。

柄の部分を親指と人差し指で挟むようにして持ち、中指で支えます。こんな感じです。

中指、薬指、小指を軽く丸めて、小指は、紙に付けます。

そして、スケッチブックのような重くて動かないものでないときは、反対の手で、紙の端を動かないように、押さえます。そこまでわかりましたか？

では、はい、皆さん、クレヨンを握ってみてくれますか。

指に力を入れすぎないようにします。

たえちゃん、クレヨンをもう少し立ててください。

ひろし君、もう少し下の方を持ってみてください。

できましたか？

では、みんなが持っている短冊の表に、「たなばた」って書いてありますね。

なぞってみましょう。ゆっくりでいいですからね。全部ね。

How to Hold a Crayon

 Oh, Hiroshi-kun, I think not only it's hard to write a letter, it would be difficult to write a straight line or color in how you hold a crayon.

Everyone please stop writing your wishes on a streamer and watch me.

Whether it's a crayon, a paint brush or a fine marker, how you hold them are the same.

You hold them with your thumb and your index finger, and your middle finger should be supporting it. Like this.

Bend your middle, forth, and pinky finger slightly and your pinky should touch the paper.

If the paper is not heavy and thick like a sketchbook hold the paper with your opposite hand so it won't move while writing. Are you alright so far?

Now, try to hold your crayons.

Don't put too much pressure on your fingers.

Tae-chan,bring your crayon slightly up.

Hiroshi-kun,try to hold your crayon a bit lower.

Is everyone doing good?

Now, I want you to slowly trace 'Tanabata' letters in front of a streamer.

Trace the words slowly. All of them.

つくってみましょう ④ 工作編

紙を染めて色とりどりの短冊を作りましょう

注意事項
1 汚れても良い服装を保護者にお願いします。
2 染めている間、テーブルを覆う新聞紙を準備しましょう。
3 鮮やかな色を出すために食紅を使います。
4 こぼれた時のために床に敷物を準備します。

ステップ 1

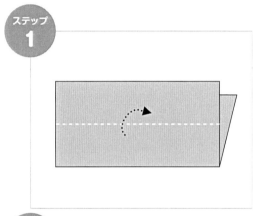

四角い紙ナプキンを準備します。優しく扱わないと破れやすいので気をつけて扱いましょう。半分に折り、もう一度半分に折ります。大きなナプキンが細長い長方形になりましたね。

Get your square paper napkin ready. Be careful with it, it can easily rip if you are not gentle enough! Fold it up in half and repeat to fold. Now, your big napkin has become a long, thin rectangle.

ステップ 2

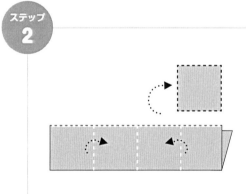

ナプキンの両端を中心線に向かって折り、さらに半分に折ります。小さな正方形を作ります。

Fold the two sides to the center line, and then fold it again in half. Your long rectangle has now become one small square.

ステップ 3

さあ、今から一番楽しいところですよ！6色の色を用意しました。やり方を良く聞いてくださいね。

Okay, now is the most interesting part! I have prepared six different colors for you. Please listen to my instructions carefully.

Let's Try ④

Tanabata Decorations
- Dyeing the Streamers -

Points to Keep in Mind

1   Contact parents to send in clothes that can get stained.
2   Prepare newspaper to cover the table while dyeing.
3   Use food coloring to create vibrant colors.
4   Prepare a clean-up rag in case of spilling.

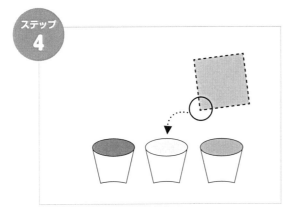

ステップ
4

ナプキンをやさしく持ち、角を一つずつ浸していきます。一つの角に2.3色混ぜてもかまいません。それから、ナプキンを気を付けて開いて、一晩乾かしましょう。

Hold your napkin gently and dip the corners into the colors one-by-one. You can mix one corner with two or three different colors. Then open it up very carefully.   Let it dry overnight.

ステップ
5

さあ、短冊を一緒に作りましょう。はじめに、ナプキンを長い長方形か三角形やひし形に切ります。もしよかったら、お友達と切った「形」を交換してもいいですよ。色々な形に切ったナプキンにボールペンで願い事を書きましょう。それからステイックのりでつなげていきましょう。

Now, let's make the 'Tanzaku' (streamer) together. First, cut the Napkin into long rectangles or shapes, such as triangles or diamonds (square turned sideways). If you like, you may trade some of your shapes with your friends. Use a ballpoint pen to write your wishes on the separate shapes. Then join the shapes together with a glue stick.

BC

つくってみましょう ⑤ 工作編

色々な七夕飾りをつくってみましょう

注意事項

前ページで染めたナプキンを使って、色々な七夕飾りを作ることができます。例を参考にして子どもたちの創造力を広げましょう。

立体的な七夕飾りを作るときにいくつか切り込み線を入れて色々なパターンを作ります。様々な大きさの紙で基本的な切り方を使って折り線も変えて試してみましょう。

染めた大きめのナプキンを選び半分に折りましょう。次のページに例が二つあります。長方形になるように半分(Example1 参照) もしくは三角形になるように半分(Example2) に折ってみましょう。

つぎに、色々なパターンの七夕飾りを作るために、いくつかの切り込みを入れていきます。必ず、口が開いていない方からのみ切り込みを入れていきます。また、紙ナプキンの半分のところで切り込みを入れるのをやめてください。さもないと、長い細い紙ができてしまいますよ。

ナプキンを開きます。筒型に丸め、角／端をのり付けします。みて！角・端をくっつけると切り込みを入れた線が小さい窓のようになって、向こうまで見えるようになるでしょ！

Using the dyed napkins you've created, there are various ways you can create the 'Tanabata Decorations.' Here are a few examples to spark your students' imagination!

Cut out some lines to create different patterns for 3D 'Tanabata Decorations .' Use the basic cutting technique on different size of paper and try to alter the folding line.

Let's select a big piece of dyed paper, fold it in half. The next page shows you the two different examples, fold it in half into a rectangle(Example 1) or triangle (Example 2).

Next, add some cut lines to make different patterns for your 'Tanabata Decorations .' Remember, you can only cut along the folded line. Also, you should stop cutting before you get to the middle of the paper. Otherwise, you will just end up with long strips of papers.

Open it up. Try to roll it into a cylinder and glue down the edge of corners. Look! If you glue the edges together, the cut lines turns into small windows, and you can see through it!

Let's Try ⑤

Tanabata Decorations

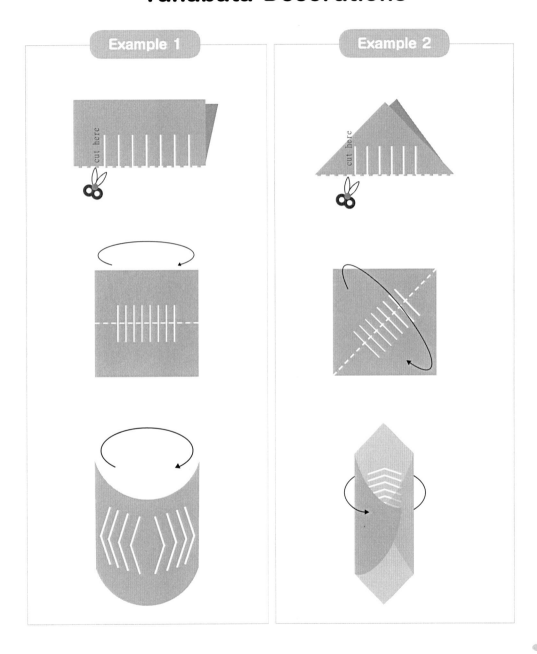

Example 1

cut here

Example 2

cut here

プール遊び

明日はプールで水遊びをする予定です。園に、水着と水泳帽、タオルとビーチサンダルをお子さまに持たせてください。

はい、ひろしもすごく楽しみにしています。水遊びが大好きですから。

そうですよね！みんな大好きです！

手足口病の流行の心配はありますか？

大丈夫そうです。今年は今のところ流行していないようです。

そうですか、それはよかったです。

うちの子は、直射日光にあたると皮膚が赤くなるんですよ。日焼け止めローションは塗ってもよいですか？

申し訳ありませんが、それはできないんです。できるだけ日陰にいるように注意しますから、それでよろしいでしょうか？

分かりました。よろしくお願いします。ひろしにも気を付けるように言っておきます。

Vocabulary

手足口病　hand, foot, and mouth disease

（病気が）広まる　go around

日光にあたる　be exposed to sunlight

日焼け止めクリーム　sunscreen

残念ですが　be afraid（that）

できるだけ　as much as possible

A Day in the Pool

We're going to play in the pool tomorrow. Please have your child bring a swim suit, a swimming cap, a towel, and beach sandals to the school.

Yes, Hiroshi is so excited. He loves to play in the water.

Of course! All kids love it!

Is there any concern about hand, foot, and mouth disease?

I don't think so. I've heard that, so far, it's not going around this year.

That's good to know.

Hiroshi's skin gets red when he is exposed to direct sun light. Is it okay if he puts on sunscreen?

I'm sorry, I'm afraid he can't. We'll try to keep him in the shade as much as possible. I hope this will be okay?

Okay. I understand. I will remind Hiroshi to be careful as well.

Point 1

put on 〜 〜が代名詞になると put 〜 on に語順が変わる日焼けする get suntanned

日焼け止めローション sunscreen

I'm afraid that 〜は、「〜 のことは残念です」、「残念ですが 〜」を表しますが、この用法では that は文章でも、口語でも省略されます。

プール遊び

明日は、みんなが大好きなプール遊びをします！

やったー！プール大好き！

明日は、水着、水泳帽、タオル、ビーチサンダルを忘れずに園に持ってきてください。

僕、鼻水がでるよ。プールに入れないっていうこと？

風邪をひいてるの？風邪をひいているようなら、プール遊びはできないわね。明日の朝、必ず熱をはかってね。

うん……。でもぼく元気だよ！

ええ、わかってるわ。明日の様子で決めましょうね、いい？

他に、風邪をひいてる人やお腹が痛い人などいませんか。

プールでこれからたくさん遊べるから、すぐには入れなくても大丈夫よ。まだこれからたくさんチャンスはあるからね、いいかな？

A Day in the Pool

Tomorrow we're going to play in the pool!

Yay! I love to play in the pool.

Don't forget to bring your swim suit, a swimming cap, a towel, and beach sandals to the school tomorrow.

I have a runny nose. Does that mean I can't go in the pool?

Do you have a cold? If you have a cold, I don't think you can play in the pool. Make sure that you take your temperature tomorrow morning, okay?

Okay, but I feel fine!

Yes, I can see that. Let's see how you are tomorrow, okay?

Does anyone else have a cold or a tummy ache?

We will play in the pool a lot from now on, so don't worry if you can't go in to the pool today, there will be lots of chances later on, okay?

プールあそびに関連する表現
Useful Phrases When Playing in the Pool

・プールではゴーグルを着けてく ださい。

・Wear swimming goggles in the pool.

・プールに飛び込まないでください。

・Don't jump into the pool.

・プールからあがったら、バスタオルで よく拭いて、お水で目を洗ってください。

・Dry off with your bath towel and wash your eyes out with fresh water after you get out of the pool.

・クロールができますか。 （平泳ぎをする、立ち泳ぎをする、背泳ぎ をする）

・Can you do the crawl? (do breaststroke, tread water, do backstroke)

・泳げない。（カナヅチです）

・He/she can't do any strokes.

つくってみましょう ⑥ おたより編

プール遊びのお知らせをしましょう（要約）

保護者各位

フォレガーデン
園長　山田　けいこ

この度、園庭で初めてのプール遊びを行いましたのでお知らせいたします。子どもたちは、午前中クラスのお友だちと水遊びを楽しみました。水を使ったゲームをしたり、友だちと自由に水遊びをしたり楽しむ様子が見られました。子どもたちは、次のプール遊びの日を楽しみにしています。

プール遊びの際、以下の点に留意してください。

1. 毎朝必ず登園前にお子様の体温を計り、連絡帳に記入してください。

2. お子様に水で遊ぶおもちゃは持たせないでください。失くしたり、壊れたり園児の間でトラブルになることがあります。

3. 雨天の場合や気温が低すぎる場合は、プール遊びは日にちを変更して行います。

ご協力お願いいたします。

Let's Try ⑥

Pool Day Report

Dear Parents,

We are happy to report that our students had their first pool day in the school yard. The children enjoyed playing with their classmates in the water throughout the morning. We had organized water-based games, and also free time to enjoy the pool with friends.

It's no surprise that the kids are already asking when the next pool day will be!

Please keep in mind the following reminders from last week's note:

1. Please take your child's temperature each morning and write it in the communication notebook.

2. Please do not send in any water toys with your child. They are easy to lose or break, and may cause arguments between students.

3. If the weather is rain or the temperature is too low, the pool day will be rescheduled.

Thank you for your understanding!

Sincerely,
Keiko Yamada, Principal
Fore Garden Preschool

鉄棒

はい、皆さん、整列して。

今日は、鉄棒の練習をしましょう。

いつも、ぶら下がって遊んでますね？

でも今から、もっとすごいことを見せますね。

先生がお手本をしますから、皆さん見ていてください。

腰を下ろして、両手は膝のところで組んでください。

良いですか、鉄棒を肩の幅よりすこし広めに両手でつかみます。

親指と他の指で、しっかりとつかみます。

つかんんだら地面を蹴って体を上に押し上げます。

体を倒して、鉄棒にお腹がかぶさるようにね。

そしたら、アゴを引いて背中をのばしたままで、クルッっと、前へ回ります。

絶対に、手を離してはだめですよ。

クルっと回ったら、足を地面につけます。

ひろし君、飛び上がる時、体が鉄棒から離れてますよ。背中を伸ばして、前に倒してください。

そして、飛び上がった時には、鉄棒から体が離れます。

そう、よくできてますよ、飛び上がって、上で止まって、ゆっくりと回って着地しますよ。

Horizontal Bar

 Okay, everyone. Please line up.

We're going to do horizontal bar exercises today.

You hang on the bar all the time while playing, right?

I'm going to show you some exciting things you can do on the bar.

Let me do a demonstration first so watch me.

Sit down and cross hands at your knees.

Okay, grab the bar at a little wider than your shoulders.

Grab tightly with your thumbs and other fingers.

Then push up your body by kicking the ground.

Slant your body and cover the bar with your stomach.

Then turn forward by pulling your chin with your back straight.

Make sure you don't let your hands off the bar.

After you flip around put your feet on the ground.

Hiroshi-kun, your body is away from the bar when you jump. You need to keep your back straight, leaning forward.

Then, when you jump, the bar will be close to your body.

Yes, you're doing well, jump, stop at the top, then slowly turn and land.

運動会の準備

😊 昨日、運動会のプログラム表を受け取りました。

保護者参加プログラムもありましたね。

😊 ええ！ぜひ、ご参加ください。

😊 綱引きでも、親子リレーでも、スプーン運びでもどれに参加してもよろしいのですか？

😊 早いもの順なんです。早くお申し込みいただければ大丈夫です。

😊 私は早く走れないので、出るなら綱引きがいいんですけど、パパが張り切っていて、自信があるといって、親子リレーに参加するのはどうですか？

😊 いいじゃないですか！ママは綱引き、パパは親子リレーではどうですか？

😊 ん…そうですね。そうしようかしら。パパには、当日ちゃんと速く走れるように、今日からジョギングするように言っておきます。

Vocabulary

エントリー（参加） participation

どれでもいい（自由に～する） be free to

綱引き tug-of-war

親子リレー parent-child relay

スプーン運び the spoon race

早いもの順 first come, first served

張り切る be keen

Getting Ready for Sports Day

We received the program for sports day yesterday.

I saw there is a parent's program.

Yes! We would love to have you join.

Am I free to join any of the events: tug-of-war, parent and child relay, or the spoon race?

Yes, it is first come, first serve. If you apply early, then you should be okay.

I can't run fast, so if I join, I would pick the tug-of-war event. That said, my husband is quite keen and pretty confident, and wants to join the parent-child relay.

That's good! How about you join the tug-of-war event and your husband joins the parent-child relay?

Hmm…okay. I'll make sure he starts jogging from today, so he can run fast enough.

Point 1

: （コロン）

前になる内容について、後ろから１）具体的な説明や言い換えをする、２）具体的に名前をあげる、３）引用文を用いる、などに用います。

; （セミコロン）

１）関連のある節を、接続詞を使わずにつなげる、２）節の間に接続副詞を用いる、
３）コンマが使われている句や節を繋げる、などに用います。

運動会の準備

もうすぐ運動会ですね。今日はみんなで運動会の予行練習をしましょう。

今日は、かけっこの練習をします。

6人ずつのグループになってスタートラインに並んでください。

では、先頭の列から順番に練習しますよ。では、位置について、よーい、ドン。

あーあ。またビリだったー！どうしたら1番になれるように速く走れるの？

一生懸命走ってるんだから、1番になるかはそんなに気にすることないのよ？でも、速くなりたかったら、毎日走る練習をするといいんじゃない？

そっか、なるほど！今日からやろうかな！そうしたら、1番になれるよね！ママきっとビックリするよね！

いいわね!楽しみだわ！みんなもがんばってね！

今日の連絡帳に、運動会のプログラムを入れましたから、お家の人に渡してくださいね？

Vocabulary

並ぶ line up

6人グループで in groups of 6

Getting Ready for Sports Day

 Sports day is coming up soon, so we're going to practice for it today.

We're going to practice running a race.

Line up at the start line in groups of 6.

Okay, we 're going to start practicing from the first row. Ready, set, go.

Oh, no. I was the last one again! How can I learn to run fast enough to be first?

Well, you're trying your best, so don't worry too much about being first. Okay? But, if you want to run faster, then you should practice running every day.

Yeah, good idea! I think I'll do that from today! Then I can be number one! My mom will be surprised!

Good. I look forward to it! Everybody, try your best!

I put the program for the sports day in your communication book, so please show it to your parents, okay?

Point 1

come up ~　~ が近づく　この意味で使う場合、進行形で使います。

Point 2

row と line

row は「横の列」、line は「縦の列 (になる)」前から 4 列目の席は、seat in the fourth row です。本文では、最初の列は「the first row」と表現しています。

運動会のお知らせを作成しよう（要約）

運動会のお知らせ

保護者各位

フォレガーデン
園長　山田　けいこ

今年も運動会の季節が近づいてきました。下記の通り運動会を開催しますので、ぜひご確認ください。

日　時　　　10月6日（土）午前9時半～午後1時

場　所　　　ガーデンパーク運動場

スケジュール　午前　9：00　　開門

　　　　　　　　　　9：30　　開会式

　　　　　　　　　　9：45　　競技開始

　　　　　　　　　11：00　　保護者競技

　　　　　　　　　12：00　　閉会式

　　　　　　　　　12：15　　昼食

　　　　　　　　　13：00　　終了

持ち物　　　体操着・運動しやすい服装・靴・帽子・水筒・お弁当

ご注意　　　1.　必ず午前9：30までに受付をしてください。

　　　　　　2.　保護者参加競技には事前に申し込みを行ってください。

　　　　　　3.　当日は十分な水分をとってください。

当日、お会いできるのを楽しみにしております。

Let's Try ⑦

A Sample Letter to Inform Parents About Sports Day

Sports Day Announcement

Dear Parents,

Fore Garden's Sports Day event is coming soon! Please review the information below to make sure you are ready for this important day.

Date & Time   Saturday, October 6th, 9:30 a.m. – 1:00 p.m.

Location   Garden Park Sports Field

Schedule

	9:00 a.m.	Doors Open
	9:30	Opening Ceremony
	9:45	Sports Events Begin
	11:00	Parent Participation Activities
	12:00 p.m.	Finishing Ceremony
	12:15	Picnic Lunch
	1:00	Finish

Things to Prepare   School gym clothes or comfortable clothing and shoes, hat, water thermos, and picnic lunch.

Reminders

1. Please check in at the reception gate before 9:30 a.m.

2. Please sign up for the parent participation activities in advance

3. Please be sure to drink plenty of water on the day

Thank you and we look forward to seeing you there!

Sincerely,
Keiko Yamada, Principal
Fore Garden Preschool

運動会

先生、おはようございます。今日は天気が良くてよかったですね。

今日は、ひろしのおばあちゃんもおじいちゃんも応援に来たんですよ。

それは素敵ですね！ひろし君も喜んでるでしょうね！だから、今日はとっても張り切っているのですね。

はじめての運動会なので、昨日はワクワクしてなかなか寝付けなかったんですよ。

ひろしがはじめに出るのは、たしか、かけっこでしたよね。

はい、プログラム3番目です。そしてその後に、大玉ころがしとダンスがお昼前にあります。

ビデオと写真を撮りたいと思ってるんですけど、保護者席がどこだかわからなくて。

プログラムはお持ちですか？最後のページを見てください。園児保護者席と記されているところです。

早めに行って席を取らないと、撮影するのにいい場所がなくなってしまいますよ。

あら、じゃあ、急がないと！

Vocabulary

〜を応援する cheer 〜 on

寝付けない can't get to sleep

プログラム3番目 third program

大玉ころがし the ball rolling relay

動画と写真を撮る take photos and video

Sports Day

Good morning, Ms. Suzuki. I'm so glad that the weather is nice today.

Hiroshi's grandparents came along to cheer their grandson on.

That's wonderful! Hiroshi-kun must be happy about that! Maybe that's why he is so excited today.

He couldn't get to sleep last night because he was too excited about his first sports day.

I believe the first program that Hiroshi will run is the short track race, right?

Yes, that event will be the third program. Then, after that is the ball rolling relay and dance just before lunch.

We'd like to take photos and a video, but I don't know where the parents' seats are located.

Do you have your program with you? Look at the back page of the program. The parents' seats are marked there.

You had better go reserve your seats, otherwise you'll miss the best spot to take your photos and video.

Ok, then we'd better hurry!

Point 1

「～をカメラで撮る」は「take the photos of ～」、「～のビデオを録る」は「record ～ on video」または「videotape ～ to」と紹介している辞書もありますが、ビデオ撮影が一般化しており、英語圏では、現在は動詞をわざわざ変えることなく、take を使うことが多いようです。

運動会

なんて良いお天気なんでしょう！運動会日和になりました！皆さんのお父さん、お母さんや家族の人もたくさん応援に来てくれました。がんばりましょうね。

おじいちゃんとおばあちゃんも来てくれたよ！

よかったわねー！おじいちゃんとおばあちゃん、頑張っているのを見て喜ぶね。

うん、一等賞とるから、後で見れるように、ビデオ撮ってねって言ったんだ。

それはよかったわね！スーパーヒーローみたいに映っているでしょうね!

でもさ…またビリだったらどうしよう？

心配しないで。だいじょうぶ！一生懸命やればいいのよ！

もうすぐ、行進が始まりますよ。先生が、足踏みはじめと言ったら、その場で足踏みを始めてくださいね。笑顔で腕を振って行進ですよ、いいですか？

さあ、立って！その場で足踏み始め！ピ！右、左、右、左。

音楽を聴いて、足踏みを続けて。右、左、右、左。

はい、全体、前へ進め。

Sports Day

What a beautiful day! It's great weather for our sports day! All your fathers, mothers, and families came to cheer for you, so please try your best.

My granddad and grandma came today!

How nice! They will be proud to see you trying so hard.

Yes, I told them that I'll be number one and that they should take a video so I can watch it later.

That's great! You'll look like a super star on the video!

But … what if I am the last one again?

Don't worry. You'll be okay! Do your best!

Soon, the marching will start. Once I say start marching, begin marching in place. Smile, swing your arms and march, okay?

Okay, stand up! Start stomping there! （whistle） Right, left, right, left.

Listen to the music, keep stomping. Right, left, right, left.

Now, everyone march forward.

運動会に関連する表現
Useful Vocabulary for Sports Day

柔軟体操	Stretching exercises	入場する	Enter the field
スプーンレース	Spoon relay race	退場する	Exit the field
障害物競争	Obstacle course	整列する	To line-up
縄跳び競争	Jump rope relay race	保護者席	Parents seats
二人三脚	Three-legged race	救護室	First-aid office
行進	Marching		

運動会のプログラム（要約）

たのしい運動会

1. 開会式（9：00）
   国旗掲揚・国歌斉唱
   園長先生のお話
   来賓の方の祝辞

2. 準備体操（ラジオ体操）　全員

3. 30メートル走　　　　　全員

4. 大玉ころがし　　　　　年長

5. ダンス　　　　　　　　年中

6. 綱引き　　　　　　　　保護者

昼食時間（12：00）

7. 親子イベント　　　　　年少親子

8. パン食い競争　　　　　卒園生

9. 玉入れ　　　　　　　　全員

10. スプーンリレー　　　　保護者と職員

閉会式

国旗降揚

Let's Try ⑧

Sports Day Program

Sports Day Program

1. Opening Ceremony
   Raising the National Flag • singing national anthem
   Principal's Opening Speech
   Visitor's Speech

2. Warm-Up Exercises（Radio Taiso）   All

3. 30 Meter Race   All

4. Ball Rolling Relay   K

5. Dance   Pre-4

6. Tug-of-War   Parents

Lunch time

7. Parent-Child Event   Parents and Pre-3

8. Snatch the Bun Race   Alumni

9. Ball Throwing Race   All

10. Spoon Relay Race   Parents & Teachers

Closing Ceremony

Taking down the National Flag

BC

単語と英語の表現 ③

運動に関連する単語
Useful Vocabulary for Exercises

腕立て伏せ	（do）push-ups
腹筋（腹筋運動）	（do）sit-ups
背筋（背筋運動）	（do）back extensions
懸垂	（do）chin-ups
逆立ち、倒立	（do）a handstand
三点倒立	（do）a headstand
側転	（do）a cartwheel

いずれも、動詞は do を用います。

（参考）「運動不足で太った。」 → Due to a lack of exercise I gained weight.

運動不足→ lack of exercise

Important Words and Phrases ③

夏季オリンピックの主な種目の英語表現
Useful Vocabulary for the Summer Olympic Games

陸上競技（Track and Field）

100m走	100-meter dash /race
110m ハードル	110-meter hurdles
走り高跳び	high jump
走り幅跳び	long jump
棒高跳び	pole vault
円盤投げ	discus throw

水泳（Swimming）

自由形	freestyle
背泳ぎ	backstroke
平泳ぎ	breaststroke
3m飛板飛び込み	3m springboard
10m高飛び込み	10m platform
バタフライ	butterfly

体操（Gymnastics）

個人総合	individual all-round
団体総合	team competition
床運動	floor exercises
鉄棒	horizontal bar
ボール平行棒	parallel bars
段違い平行棒	uneven bars
鞍馬	pommel horse
跳馬	vault
吊り輪	rings
平均台	balance beam

球技（Ball Sports）

サッカー	soccer
バレーボール	volleyball
卓球	table tennis

BC

知ってると、ちょっとスマートな英語表現②

「Please ～ .」と「I need you to ～ .」

「please」がついていると、丁寧な言い方に聞こえますが、強い口調で言うと相手に指示・命令しているように聞こえます。「Please turn off the lights!」と言うと、「電気を消してください」ではなく「お願いだから電気を消してくれ！いつもつけっ放しなんだから！」という意味の表現になります。

これでは、ケンカになりかねません。

優しくお願いしたい時も命令したい時も、「need」を用いるのがお勧めです。「I need you to turn off the lights.」というと「電気を消してほしいんだけど。（いいかな？）」とやんわりとした表現になります。

「You're wrong.」と「You might need to rethink that.」

英語の授業で、「あなたは間違っています。」の英訳は「You 're wrong.」と習いませんでしたか？これは間違いではありませんが、この表現は、すごく強く否定、非難された感じになってしまいますので、会話ではあまりおすすめする言い方ではありません。

「You might need to rethink that.」と表現します。「ちょっと違うかもしれないから考えなおしてみたら。」というニュアンスで、相手からも「Oh, thank you. I'll try!」と言われスムーズでフレンドリーな会話になります。

「I forgot.」と「It slipped my mind.」

英語の授業で「忘れました。」の英訳を「I forgot.」と習います。

間違いではありませんが、何か忘れ物をしたときに「どうしたの？」と聞かれて「I forgot.」というと、口調にもよりますが、「忘れたけど、だからどうなのよ。」と開き直った表現にもなります。

「うっかり忘れてしまいました。すいません。」というニュアンスにしたいときは、「slipped」を使い、「It slipped my mind.」という表現をおすすめします。

第3章　楽しい園の行事 ②
（秋から冬）

Chapter 3　Fun School Events ②
（Fall 〜 Winter）

第2章に引き続き、秋から冬にかけての行事を取上げて、英会話の表現を学習します。
この時期は行事も多く、ますます楽しみも多くなります。

発表会準備

おはようございます。昨日、発表会のお知らせをいただきました。

ママ達が衣装作り頑張らないといけないんですね！

おはようございます。ええ！大変だとは思いますがご協力よろしくお願いします。

子どもたちの配役が決まったら、色や材料など衣装づくりの詳細を教えていただけますか？

はい。詳細が決まったらお知らせします。

いつまでに衣装を作ればよいのか期日は決まっていますか？

はい。発表会の３日前に、衣装をきてリハーサルをおこなうので、そのときまでにはでき上がっていて欲しいです。

わかりました。このような大きな催しものですと、誰が何をやるのか役を決めるのは大変ですよね。

みんなが自分の子に主役をやらせたいと思うでしょうから。みんなが納得できるようにするのはなかなか難しいでしょうね。

Vocabulary

発表会 the school performance

衣装 costume

〜より前に prior to 〜

役 cast

主役 the main cast

Preparing for Performance Day

Good morning. Yesterday we received the letter with the information about the school performance.

It says that the moms have to make the children's costumes!

Good morning. Yes! It's pretty challenging, but we appreciate your cooperation.

Once you decide on the cast, will you let us know further details about the costumes, like which colors and what types of material to use?

Yes. Once we have more specific information, we'll let you know.

Have you set a deadline for when you want the costumes finished?

Yes. We will have a dress rehearsal three days prior to the performance date, so all the costumes need to be done by then.

Okay. It must be challenging to decide who does what on such a big project.

Many of the parents probably want their kids to be in the main cast. I am sure it is difficult to make everyone happy.

Point 1

make everyone happy. みんなを平等にする

「公平に」という「fair」を用いず、「全員が幸せになる」ということで表現しています。
この表現は英語圏らしい表現です。

発表会準備

 もうすぐ、発表会があります。みんなのお父さん・お母さんや家族の人をお呼びして、クラスのお遊戯や劇を見てもらいます！

このクラスでは、みんなが大好きな「星座になったクマの物語」を英語でやります。まずは、役から決めましょうね。

好きな役をやっていいの？

みんなが好きな役をやったら、ケンカになったり、誰もやりたくない役が出ちゃうわね。

どうやって決めたらいいか誰かいい案ないかな？

じゃんけんは？

そうね、じゃんけんで決めてもいいわね、でも時間がかかるわね。くじ引きで決めるのはどう？

先生が、袋の中に役が書いてある紙を入れるから、一人ずつとってくれる？そうすれば、みんな公平に決められるんじゃない かしら？

Vocabulary

役（配役）を決める pick the cast members

くじ引きをする draw

公平な fair

（＊会話文1-1では、‘make everyone happy’ という表現も紹介しています）

Preparing for Performance Day

  The school performance day is coming soon. We'll invite your fathers, mothers and families to see our school dance and performance!

We are going to perform "The Story of a Bear Who Became a Star" in English. Everyone's favorite story, so let's begin by picking the cast members.

  Can I play any character that I want to be?

  Well, if everybody picks who they want to be, then there could be a fight, or we might have a character that no one wants to be.

Does anyone have a good idea how best to choose the parts for the play?

  How about rock, paper, scissors?

  Hmm…we could do that, but it takes time. How about we draw names?

I'll put a piece of paper with all the character's names in a bag, and you each take one, okay? This is a fair way to decide, don't you think?

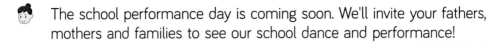

Point 1

発表会で使える単語の紹介

演者 cast　　　　　　主役 leading role　　　　脇役 supporting role

セリフ line　　　　　　衣装 costume　　　　　　舞台 stage

照明 lighting　　　　　音響 sound

発表会のお知らせを作成しよう（要約）

発表会のお知らせ

保護者各位

来る12月12日に、毎年恒例の発表会を行います。

今年は、はじめて英語劇に取り組みました。

子どもたちが初めて外国語で行う演技に温かい応援をお願いいたします。

来週配役を決めます。保護者の皆様には衣装制作をお願いいたします。

ご協力よろしくお願いいたします。

発表会の劇

クラス	ウサギ組（年中組）
担任	鈴木　よしこ
タイトル	星座になったクマの物語
時間	20分
物語	有栖川山に住む動物たちはとても仲良しでした。なぜなら力持ちで優しいクマさんパパがいつも守ってくれていたからです。ある日突然起きた火災で、大変な事になりました…。
ねらい	園児たちの英語力上達と熱心な演技

うさぎ組　担任　鈴木　よしこ

Let's Try ⑨

Information About Annual Performance Day

Information About Our Annual Performance Day

Dear Parents,

We will have our annual Performance Day on December 12th.

The children will be performing a play in English this year for the first time.

Please give a warm cheer to the children for practicing so hard to be able to perform in a foreign language.

We are going to select the cast next week. We would like to ask parents to make their child's costume.

We appreciate your cooperation.

Sincerely,
Yoshiko Suzuki

Information About the Play the Children will Perform

Class	:	Rabbit Class (Pre-4)
Teacher	:	Yoshiko Suzuki
Title	:	The Story of a Bear Who Became a Star
Time	:	20 minutes
Story	:	All the animals living in Arisugawayama were very friendly because there was a powerful and kind Papa Bear who was always looking after them. Suddenly, there was a fire and it caused a terrible tragedy.
Areas to Notice	:	Children's progress learning English and their energetic performance.

BC

発表会

お母さん、素晴らしい衣装を作って頂いてありがとうございました。毎日お忙しいのに、さぞかし大変だったでしょう！

そんなことはないですよ。先生も園で大変でしょう！何か私でお役に立てることがあれば喜んでしますよ。ひろしも家で頑張って何度も自分のセリフを練習していました。

それはすごいですね！ひろしくんの役はセリフが多いので、ちょっと緊張してると思いますよ。

ひろしの祖父母を紹介します。ひろしが電話をして、今日はおじいちゃん、おばあちゃんに見に来てもらったんですよ。

こんにちは、はじめまして。ひろし君の担任の鈴木です。今日はお越しいただきありがとうございます。

はじめまして。よく、ひろしからお話は聞いています。先生のこと大好きなようで。今日はとっても楽しみです！

Vocabulary

手伝う help out

なんでも in any way

緊張している be nervous

セリフが多い have a lot to say

Performance Day

Thank you for making such a nice costume. I know you are busy every day and it must have been quite difficult for you to manage it!

Not at all. You are also working so hard here at school! I am happy to help out in any way I can. Hiroshi has been practicing very hard every day for this part.

That's wonderful! He has a lot to say so he must be a bit nervous.

I would like to introduce Hiroshi's grandparents. He called and asked them to come and see him perform today.

Hello, nice to meet you. I'm Suzuki, Hiroshi-kun's homeroom teacher. Thank you for coming today.

Nice to meet you, too. I have heard a lot about you from Hiroshi. He really likes you. We are excited to be here today!

Point 1

「手伝う」の単語の使い分け help は積極的に必要な援助をすること、aid は救済する場合、assist は、補助的な手伝いをすることを表します。

発表会

 今日はいよいよ、発表会の本番ですね。みんな緊張しているかな？

沢山の人が来てる！緊張して胸がドキドキするな。セリフを全部、覚えているといいんだけど。

心配ないわ。何度も練習したから、大丈夫よ。大きくてしっかりとした声でセリフを言うことを忘れないでね。

間違えちゃったらどうしよう？？

心配しないで、大丈夫よ。お友だちがセリフを忘れたときは教えて助けてあげてね。

がんばればいいんだもんね？

そうよ、一生懸命やったらいいのよ。失敗してもくよくよしなくていいのよ。そのまま続ければいいのよ！

じゃあ、ステージに行きましょうか？

音楽スタート！

Performance Day

It's performance day. Are you all nervous?

There are many people here! I'm so nervous, and I feel like I have butterflies in my stomach. I hope I remember all my lines.

Don't worry. We had plenty of rehearsals, so I am sure you will be fine. Remember to speak your lines in a loud, strong voice.

What if I make a mistake?

Don't worry. You will be fine. If your friends forget their part, then try to help them out, okay?

Just do our best, right?

Yes, do your best. There's nothing to feel uneasy about if you make mistakes. Just keep on going!

Okay, shall we get ready for the stage?

Let's start the music!

Vocabulary

胸がドキドキする have butterflies in one's stomach

リハーサル rehearsal

せりふ line

せりふを言う speak lines

不安な uneasy

～したらどうなる？ What if ～

かんむりをつくりましょう

ステップ 1

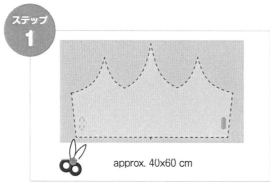

approx. 40x60 cm

長い紙に印刷されている線に沿って切って
いきましょう。頭のサイズを測りましょう。
両面テープを使い後で端をとめます。

Cut along the dotted line printed on the
long strip of paper. Measure the crown
on your head. Use double-sided tape to
fix the edges together later.

ステップ 2

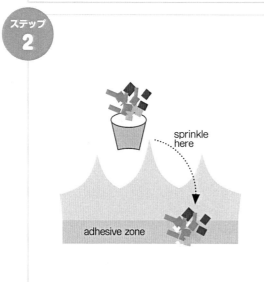

sprinkle here

adhesive zone

薄紙や古い包装紙を小さくちぎりましょ
う。床に落とさないようにしましょう。ち
ぎった紙を小さな入れ物に入れるのを忘れ
ずに。線を描くように、スティックのりを
使ってかんむりの下部にのりを付けます。
それから、ちぎった紙をかんむりの下部の
接着部にちりばめます。

Tear up some tissue paper or
recycled wrapping paper into tiny
pieces. Please try not to drop them
on the floor. Remember to put all the
tiny pieces in a small cup. Use a glue
stick to cover the bottom area of your
crown, like drawing a line with the
glue. Then, sprinkle the ripped-up
pieces of paper onto the adhesive
zone at the bottom of your crown.

ステップ 3

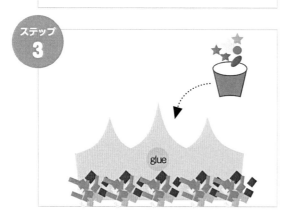

glue

では、かんむりのスパンコールをちりばめ
たいところにスティックのりを付けていき
ます。今度はのりで線を描くのではなく、
丸を描きましょう。それからちぎった紙の
ときと同じ手順で新たな接着部にちりばめ
ましょう。

Now, apply your glue stick to a different
area of the crown where you want to
add the sequins. This time, you can
draw a circle instead of a line. Then
doing the same procedure as with the
ripped-up tissue paper, sprinkle them
onto the new adhesive zone.

Let's Try ⑩

Making a Crown

ステップ 4

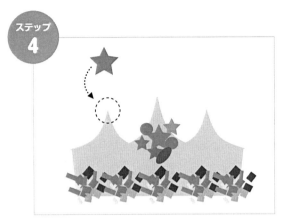

3つの星を選んで、かんむりのとがったところに、糊付けしましょう。ラメをさらにつけてかざってもいいです。

Take three stars and glue them on top of each tip of the crown. If you like, you can add some glitter.

ステップ 5

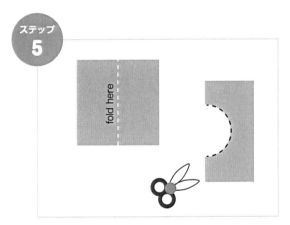

fold here

最後にかんむりの両側を二つの切り抜きを作って飾ります。折り紙を半分に折り、折ったところから半円を切りましょう。

For the last step, we will make two stencils to decorate both sides of the crown. Fold a square origami sheet in half and cut out a half circle from the folded line, then open it up.

ステップ 6

真ん中に丸い穴ができましたね。折り紙を回転させてダイヤモンドの形にして、冠に貼りましょう。見て！穴からかんむりの色が見えるでしょ？これで完成！

Now, you have a hole in the middle of the paper. Turn the origami sheet around and make a diamond shape. Glue it down on both sides of the crown. Look! See how the color of the crown will show up inside the circle. Now, you're done!

BC

英語劇　星座になったクマの物語 （脚本 書き出し部分）

ナレーター	「有栖川山に住む動物たちはとても仲良しでした。
	それは、とても優しく、頼もしいクマさんパパがいたからです。
	クマさんパパには坊やがいました。
	クマさんママは坊やを生んだときに死んでしまいました。
	ある日の夜、大きな山火事が起きました。」
舞台転換	（リスさん達が寝床で寝ている。舞台中央　舞台袖から火の手が上がる）
リス①	「起きてー。なにかパチパチした音と煙のにおいがする！」
リス②	「わ！火事だ！逃げなきゃ！でもみんなまだ寝てるよ！」
リス③	「おサルさんパパにどうしたらいいか聞いてみよう！」
リス①②	「そうしよう、そうしよう。行って聞いてみよう。」
舞台転換	（リス③ステージ左手の木の上のはしごに座っているおサルさんパパへ走る。）
リス③	「おさるさんパパ、おさるさんパパ、起きてください！火事です！」
おサルさんパパ	「何？　大変だ！　火事はどこ？」
	「本当だ！まだ安全なところに逃げられる。行こう！」
おサルさんママ	「行きましょう。みんな森の仲間たちは寝ているわ、手分けしてみんなを起こしましょう。」
おサルさんたち	「そうしよう！みんなを起こそう！早く、手分けして起こさなきゃ！」

ABC

The Story of a Bear Who Became a Star

（シナリオ書き出しのシーン）

（ご希望の大学、短大、専門学校、高校、中学、小学校、幼稚園、保育園には本劇のシナリオ全編を差し上げます。尚、本シナリオによる劇を行われた場合には、そのビデオのご提供をお願いいたします。当協会のホームページ等にて公開させて頂きたいと思います）

The Story of a Bear Who Became a Star

Squirrel ①	Wake up! I hear crackling sound and smell smoke!
Squirrel ②	Oh! It's a fire! We had better escape! But everybody is still sleeping!
Squirrel ③	Let's ask Papa Monkey what to do!
Squirrel ①②	Good idea, good idea. Let's go and ask him.
（Stage Directions）	All squirrels run to the Papa Monkey, who is sitting on a ladder decorated to look like a tree on the left side of the stage
Squirrel ③	Papa Monkey, wake up! There's a fire!
Papa Monkey	What! Oh, no! Where is the fire?
	I can see it! I think we still have time to get to safety. Let's go!
Mama Monkey	Let's go. Everyone in the forest is still sleeping, so let's spread out and try to wake them up.
All monkeys	Yes! Let's go wake everyone! Quickly, let's spread out and wake them up!

餅つき大会

本日はお手伝いに来て頂き、ありがとうございます。

いいえ。私もお手伝いするのは好きですから。

餅つきなんて何年ぶりかしら。一番上の子が生まれて最初のお正月以来だから、5年ぶりくらいです。

そうなんですか？では、やったことがあるのですか？それは心強いです！

いえいえ、お役に立つかどうか。もしかしたら、食べるだけの係になってしまうかも！

だいじょうぶですよ！今日は、お父様方が園長とお餅をついてくださるので、お母様方には、餅米を蒸すのと丸めてもらうお手伝いをお願いします。

いいですよ！お任せください、お餅を丸めます。

ありがとうございます。お餅をこねるのは、子どもたちにお手伝いさせます。

お餅の中にあんこを入れるのは難しいので、お餅のまわりに、きな粉をまぶします。

Vocabulary

お手伝い　volunteer

（餅を）つく　pound

～を蒸す　steam ～

こねる　knead

最後には～で終わる　end up ～ ing

餅米　glutinous rice

～丸める　roll ～

Omochitsuki Event

Thank you for coming to help us today.

Not at all. I like to volunteer.

I haven't done mochitsuki for a long time. It's been five years since the last time I did it during the new year when my oldest child was born.

Really? So, you have experienced doing this? That's great!

I don't know how helpful I will be though. Maybe I will just end up eating it!

Oh don't worry. The principal and dads will pound the mochi today, so we would like to ask the moms to steam and roll the mochi.

Great! I'm sure I can handle that, and I'm happy to roll mochi.

Thank you. We'll let the kids help knead the mochi.

It may be difficult to put anko in the mochi, so we'll cover it with some kinako.

Point 1

It's been five years since the last time I did it ⋯

直訳すると「最後にそれをしてから5年になる。」ですが、「それをするのは〜以来5年ぶりだ。」と言う表現と捉えることができます。また、英語で「久しぶりだ」は、It's been a long time. と言います。

お餅つきを説明してみましょう

Mochitsuki (Rice Pounding)

お正月の前後に、もち米を蒸して、臼に入れ、杵でつき、様々な形にした餅を作ります。

During the final day of the year and at the beginning of each new year, glutinous rice (mochi-rice) is steamed, dumped into a wooden bowl (an usu), and pounded with a kine (like a wooden hammer). It is then flattened and made into delicious, smooth, and shiny mochi.

79

餅つき大会

明日は、餅つき大会をおこないます。楽しそうだと思わない？

餅つきをやったことがある人いる？

はーい！おじいちゃんの家でやりました。

それはいいわね。みんな、どうやってお餅をつくか知ってる？

餅米を臼という木でできた大きなボウルにいれるの。それで杵という大きな木のカナヅチのようなものでお米をついて、なめらかに平らにするのよ。

ついていくうちに、だんだんネバネバしたお餅になっていくのです。

お餅、食べられるの？

もちろんです。明日はお父さんたちがきて、お餅をつくのを手伝ってくれるので、みんなでお餅を丸めて、きな粉をつけたり、小豆等を入れたりして、おいしいお餅をつくりましょう。

作り終わったら、一緒に食べましょう！

おいしそう！一個以上食べていいの？

いいわよ。でもあんまり食べるとお腹が痛くなっちゃうからね。
それと、あまり慌てて飲み込んではいけませんよ、のどにつまってしまいますから。

Omochitsuki Event

 Tomorrow's Omochitsuki day. Doesn't that sound like fun?

Has anyone done this before?

Yeah! I did it at my grandad's house.

That's nice. Does everybody know how to pound mochi rice to make rice cakes?

We take the mochi rice and put it into a big wooden bowl（an usu）. Then use like a wooden hammer（a kine）and pound the mochi rice to make it smooth and flat.

When you pound the mixture the mochi rice gradually changes to sticky mochi.

Can we eat it?

Yes, of course. Tomorrow your fathers will come to help us pound the mochi rice, so you can roll it out and put kinako（roasted soy bean flour）and azuki beans inside to make them yummy.

Once we've made them let's eat them together!

Yummy! Can we eat more than one?

Yes, but try not to eat too much or you'll get a stomachache. Finally, don't swallow too quickly to avoid getting it stuck in your throat.

Vocabulary

楽しそうだと思わない？（反語）Doesn't that sound like fun?

ネバネバした　sticky

丸める　roll-up

きな粉　roasted soy bean flour

小豆　red beans

餅つき大会のボランティア参加をお願いする書面を作ってみましょう（要約）

餅つき大会ボランティア参加のお願い

保護者各位

フォレガーデン
園長　山田　けいこ

1月25日（金）に、餅つき大会を開催します。職員・子ども達・保護者の皆様と協力しながら、伝統的なお餅を作りましょう。

餅つきは楽しいのですがその分仕事もたくさんあります。当日、大会を円滑に進めるために保護者の皆様にご協力をお願いします。お手伝い頂ける時間を下記に記入し、用紙を1月11日（金）までに園に提出願います。

------------------------------ 切り取り線 ------------------------------

園児名: _____　　　クラス: _____

保護者名: _____

ご協力いただける保護者の方は、ご都合のよい時間を一つ選んで、印をつけてください。

時間	担当業務
□9:30-10:00 a.m.	準備
□10:00-10:30	餅つき
□10:30-11:00	餅つき
□11:00-11:30	餅つき
□11:30-12:00 p.m.	昼食
□12:00-1:00	片づけ

□当日ボランティアに参加できません。

Let's Try ⑪

A Call for Volunteers

A Call for Volunteers

Dear Parents,

Friday, January 25th will be our mochitsuki event. Staff, children, and the parents will work together to make these delicious, traditional rice cakes.

Mochitsuki is a lot of fun, but also a lot of work. We need all families to volunteer for one time slot to help make this event successful. Please fill out the survey below and return it to the school by Friday, January 11th.

Sincerely,
Keiko Yamada, Principal
Fore Garden Preschool

------------------------------ please cut here ------------------------------

Child's Name: _____ Child's Class: _____

Volunteer Parent Name: _____

Please check one of the following volunteer time slots:

Time	Duty
☐ 9:30-10:00 a.m.	Preparation
☐ 10:00-10:30	Mochitsuki
☐ 10:30-11:00	Mochitsuki
☐ 11:00-11:30	Mochitsuki
☐ 11:30-12:00 p.m.	Lunch
☐ 12:00-1:00	Clean-up
☐ I am unable to volunteer on this day.	

節分

 ひろし、今日は鬼の役をしたの？鬼のお面、よく似合ってるわね。

えぇ、そうなんです。ひろし君の鬼の役、よかったですよ。

あら、楽しそうね。

オニをやりたい人がいるかクラスのみんなに聞いたら、ひろし君が真っ先に手を挙げてくれたんですよ。

豆まきの時もとっても大きな声を出してくれたんですよ。

ひろしは、行事が大好きなんです。

はい、そのようですね。自分だけが楽しむのではなく、みんなのことも楽しませてくれるんです。

だから、クラスでも人気者なんですよ。

そう、ひろし、よかったわね！

Vocabulary

～を楽しませるのが得意 be good at entertaining

～大きな声をあげる raise one's voice

Setsubun

Did you pretend to be a demon today? You look great in the demon mask.

Yes, he did. He was a great demon.

Wow, that sounds very exciting.

We asked members of the class, who wanted to be a demon, and Hiroshi-kun raised his hand immediately.

He raised his voice loudly when we threw the beans too.

Hiroshi loves all the festival activities.

Yes, I can see that. Not only does he enjoy himself, but he's also good at entertaining others.

So, he's also popular in the class.

Wow, that's great Hiroshi!

Point 1

節分について説明してみましょう

Coming of Spring（Setsubun）

2月3日に、「鬼は外、福は内」と言って豆をまき、新しい年の幸福を願います

On February 3, children throw beans and chant, "Oni wa soto, Fuku wa uchi"（Demon（bad luck）out, happiness in）to wish for happiness and good luck for the new year.

Point 2

Not only ~ , but also …

文頭に否定語が出ている場合、倒置が起きるので、Does he enjoy himself のように do（does, did）＋主語＋本動詞の語順になります。

節分

今日は 2 月 3 日ですね。何の日か知っていますか？

今日は豆をまいて、悪い運を追い出す日だよね！

そうですね！節分、って言います。

節分は家の中から外へ、それから家の外から中へ「鬼は外、福は内」と叫びながら豆をまきます。悪い運を追い出して、福を招くという意味ですよね。

園でも豆まきをおこないます。

いつもは、鬼のお面を作って、みんなの中から鬼の役を一人選んで、鬼役の子に鬼のお面をかぶってもらいます。

ほかのみんなは、鬼役の子に豆を投げて、鬼を怖がらせて悪いことを追い出します。

僕、鬼はいやだなー。豆をぶつけられると痛いし。

あら、そんなことはないわよ、痛くなんかないわよ。それにね、鬼の役をした子は、一年を通してすごくいいことがあると、昔からの言い伝えがあるのよ！

先生がそう言うならじゃあ、僕、鬼やる！

Vocabulary

〜を取り除く　get rid of 〜

一年を通して　throughout the year

豆まきをする　throw beans

言い伝え　saying

Setsubun

Today is February 3rd. Do you know what is special about today?

Today is the day when we throw beans to get rid of any bad luck around us!

That's right! It's called Setsubun.

In Setsubun, we throw beans from the inside of the house to the outside, and then from the outside of the house to the inside, while shouting "Oni wa soto! Fuku wa uchi!", which means, "Bad luck out! Good fortune in!", right?

We also throw beans at school.

Usually we make a demon mask and we choose one person in the class to be a demon and have that person wear a demon mask.

Then, the rest of the class throws beans at that person to scare the demon, or bad luck away.

I don't want to be a demon. It'll hurt if I get beans thrown at me.

Oh, please don't worry, it doesn't hurt. We have a saying from a long time ago that whoever plays the demon will have good luck throughout the year!

Well, if you say that, then I'll do it!

Point 1

「鬼」を使った日本のことわざで鬼が表現されない英語表現

鬼が出るか蛇が出るかわからない　There's no knowing what terrifying thing may happen.

来年のことを言うと鬼が笑う　Nobody [Only God] knows what may happen next year.

鬼の居ぬ間に洗濯　When the cat's away, the mice will play.

鬼の目にも涙　Even the hardest heart will sometimes be moved to pity.

つくってみましょう ⑫ 工作編

豆入れを作りましょう

ステップ 1

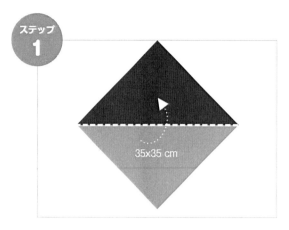

画用紙寸法：35cm × 35cm。

画用紙を三角形になるように半分に折ります。

Get your construction paper (size: 35cm × 35cm) ready, then fold it in half to make a triangle.

ステップ 2

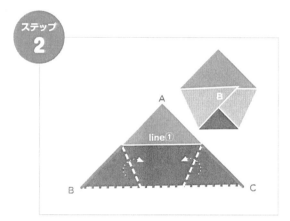

A を下向きに折り開きます。できた折り目を (line①) とします。次に B を上に折り line①に合わせます。C も同様に折ります。

Fold down A and then open it up. Now, you will see a line there, let's call it 'line①'. Fold up B to match line①. Repeat the step with B and C.

ステップ 3

A の上の1枚を下に折り、カップの形にします。これが鬼の胴体部になります。

Fold down the top front triangle (A) to create a cup (Demon's body).

How to Make a Bean Bag

ステップ
4

25x35 cm

胴体部ができたので、オニの顔の部分を作ります。

顔面部（赤色長方形1枚　25cm × 35cm）、角部（黄色三角形2枚：大）、鼻、牙（白色三角形3枚）、髪の毛（黒い毛糸）、目（白色大円形2枚、黒色小円形2枚）

準備はいいですか？

Now, that you have the body parts ready, let's make your demon's face.

Face （1 red paper rectangle: 25cm × 35cm）, horns （2 big-sized yellow triangles）, nose and teeth （3 small-sized white triangles）, hair （some black pieces of yarn）, eyes （2 big and white and 2 small black circles）

Everybody ready?

ステップ
5

顔面部にそれぞれのパーツを貼り付けて、鬼の顔を作ります。黒い毛糸を鬼の髪に使います。黒のマジックペンで口を描きます。

Let's glue all the shapes to create the face. Use the black yarn for the hair. For the mouth, draw it with a black marker.

ステップ
6

最後にステップ3で作った胴体と合体させます。胴体部の A の三角の部分に鬼の顔を糊付けします。出来上がったら、胴体部のカップに豆を入れましょう。これで出来上がりです。

Let's stick the head to the body we made in Step 3. Glue the head down on A. Now, let's fill it up with beans. You are done!

BC

節分のお面を作りましょう

ステップ 1

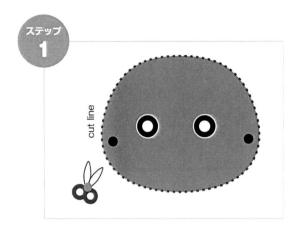

cut line

今日は節分の鬼のお面をつくります。点線に沿って鬼の顔を丁寧に切り抜きましょう。

Today we are going to make a Demon Mask. Please follow the dotted line carefully to cut the face out first.

ステップ 2

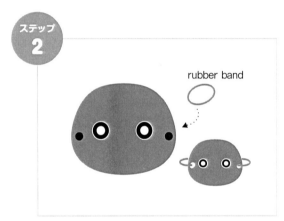

rubber band

パンチで●印のところに二つ穴をあけ、ゴムを通します。

Use a hole punch to cut out two small holes where the black dots are to make holes for a rubber band to go through.

ステップ 3

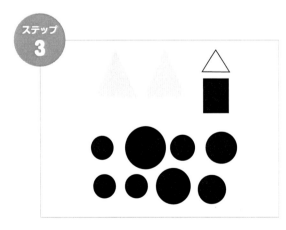

では、サイズの違う黒い丸形を数枚、黄色2枚と白色1枚の三角形を準備しましょう。

黒の折り紙を半分に切って、長方形にして準備しておきましょう。鬼の顔のパーツになります。

Now, prepare some black circles in different sizes, two yellow triangles, a white triangle, and a black rectangle-shaped origami paper. These will be the parts of the demon's face.

Let's Try ⑬

How to Make a Demon Mask

ステップ 4

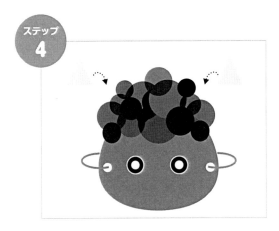

サイズの違う黒い丸を重ねて、面白い髪形を作りましょう。角には、黄色い三角形をふたつ使います。髪の毛の上に貼りましょう。

Overlap the black circles to make a funny hair style. For his horns, use two yellow triangles, and glue them on top of the hair.

ステップ 5

小さい白い三角形を小さく2枚に切り、牙をつくります。口はマジックペンで描きましょう。

For the teeth, cut a small white triangle into 2 small pieces. For the mouth draw a line with a marker.

ステップ 6

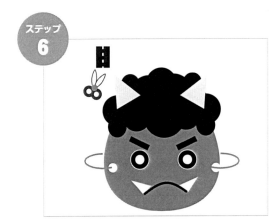

最後のステップです。黒い長方形の折り紙を半分に切ります。これが眉毛の部分になります。怖い顔になるように眉尻をそれぞれ違う方向に傾け、眉毛にしてみましょう。

This is the last step. Fold a small piece of black origami paper and cut it in half. These are going to be your demon's eyebrows. Try to turn the eyebrows in different directions to find the scariest look!

BC

ひなまつり

今日のお昼はとってもおいしいチラシ寿司だったんですね。

はい、子どもたちにも大好評でした。おかわりする子も多くて、すぐになくなってしまいました！

それはよかったですね。あら、ひろし、かわいいひな人形の折り紙もつくったのね。ママに見せて？

かわいいと思いませんか？ひろし君、きちんと折れるように一生懸命でしたよ。作るのが結構難しいんですけど、最後まで諦めないで、きれいな折り紙のひな人形を作ったんですよ。

おうちで、おひなさまを飾ってらっしゃるそうですね。

そうなんですよ。ひろしは男の子ですが、今は女の子もいるので、飾っているんですよ。

そうですか。お嬢さんは確か…

はい、もうすぐ6カ月になります。おすわりができるようになりました。おひなさまの前で写真を撮るのを楽しみにしているんです！

まあ、かわいい！お家でひな祭りがお祝いできて良いですね。女の子はこの日が大好きですから。

そうなんです、母と私はようやくこの楽しい日がお祝いできてうれしく思っています。

Vocabulary

おかわりをする ask for seconds

かわいいと思いませんか？ Aren't they cute? （反語）

我慢する persevere（＝put up with）

飾る put out

Hinamatsuri

I heard you served very delicious chirashi-zushi today.

Yes, the children seemed to really enjoy it. We had several children asked for seconds and we quickly ran out!

How wonderful. Oh, Hiroshi, you made pretty origami hina dolls too. Can you show them to mama?

Aren't they cute? Hiroshi-kun worked very hard to fold them just right. They are difficult to make, but he persevered and made beautiful origami dolls.

I heard that you display hina dolls at home.

Yes. I have a boy, but now I also have a daughter, so we put them out for her.

I see. Your girl is…

She's almost 6 months. She's able to sit up on her own now. I am looking forward to taking her picture in front of the hina doll display!

How cute. It's great that you can celebrate Hinamatsuri at home. Girls love that day.

Yes, my mother and I are very happy that we can finally celebrate this fun holiday.

Point 1

園で使える put を用いたイディオム

put on　　　身につける (※wearは着ている状態、put on は着る動作を指します)

put ～ away　～を片づける　　　put your toys away (おもちゃを片づけなさい)

put ～ back　(元の所に)～を戻す　　put the book back　(絵本を元の場所に戻して)

put ～ down　下に置く　　　　　put the crayon down　(クレヨンを下において)

put ～ together　～を組み立てる　　put toys together　(おもちゃを組み立てる)

put up with ～　～を我慢する　　put up with a toothache　(歯が痛いのを我慢する)

ひなまつり

 今日は３月３日です。何の日か知っていますか？

ひな祭り！女の子の日！

あら、ひろし君、よく知ってるわね。

だって、妹が生まれたからママがおひなさまを飾ってたもの。

そうね、女の子のいるうちではおひなさまを飾って、甘酒を飲んで、色とりどりの雛あられを食べます。

チラシ寿司も食べるんでしょ？

そうですね。今日のお昼ごはんは、なんとチラシ寿司よ。みんな好きだと思うわ。

Hinamatsuri

 Today is March 3rd. Do you know what is special about today?

It's Hinamatsuri! It's the girl's festival.

Oh, you know well, Hiroshi-kun.

Yeah, because now I have a baby sister, and my mom put hina dolls on display.

Yes, if you have a girl in your house, you put hina dolls on display, drink sweet sake, and eat colorful hina rice crackers.

We also eat chirashi-zushi, right?

Yes. In fact, we will have chirashi-zushi for lunch today. I'm sure you'll like it.

Point 1

ひなまつりについて説明してみましょう。

3月3日は、女の子の幸せと健康を祈ってお祝いする日です。とくに、女の子が生まれた最初の節句は大切です。自宅に雛人形やお祝いのかざり飾りつけをしてお客様を招いて招いてごちそうでもてなします。雛人形は、前もって飾っておき、3月3日当日に片付けるのが大切とされています。3月3日を過ぎて飾っていると結婚が遠のくと言われています。

On March 3rd, we celebrate the Doll Festival by making wishes for the good health and happiness of girls. Especially when a baby girl is born, the 1st sekku, or event, is important. We display hina dolls, make festival dishes, and invite people over to our houses to create a festive spirit around the girls in the house. It is important to display hina dolls well in advance of the actual event, and then be sure to pack away the dolls on March 3rd. People say that if you display the hina dolls after March 3rd, the girl's marriage will be delayed.

おひなさまを作りましょう

ステップ 1

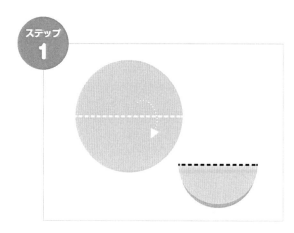

今日はおひなさまを作ります。

紙皿を準備して、半分に折ります。

これがおひなさまの体の部分になります。

Today we are going to create O-hina-sama.

Okay, get your paper plates ready and then fold them in half. These are going to be their bodies.

ステップ 2

The Prince's Hat　The Princess's Crown

Face　Face

顔を作ります。気をつけてはさみで、線に沿って顔と烏帽子（えぼし）とかんむりを画用紙から切り取ります。

Now, we will work on their faces. Hold the scissors carefully and, following the line, cut out their faces, the Prince's hat and the Princess's crown from construction paper.

ステップ 3

色鉛筆でおひなさまの目、鼻、口と髪の毛を描きます。おひなさまのほっぺに少しピンク色を入れることを忘れずに。

はい！でき上がり。なんて2人ともかわいらしいのでしょう！

Then, get your colored pencils ready, as we are going to draw their eyes, noses, mouths and hair.

Don't forget to add some pink on the Princess's cheek.

Wow, look how sweet they are!

Let's Try ⑭

Hinamatsuri Doll Crafts

ステップ 4

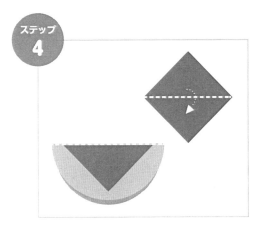

次に、折り紙を使って、着物を着せていきます。

折り紙をひし形になるように持ち、半分におります。

三角の部分を下にして半分に折った紙皿に重ねて挟みます。手順を繰り返し、二人分の着物をつくります。

Next, we will use a piece of origami paper for the kimono to dress them up! Hold your origami paper like a diamond and fold it in half. Turn the triangle tip face down, keep the folded part on top, and use it to cover the top of the paper plate.

Repeat the step to make the prince's kimono.

ステップ 5

2人の顔の部分と着物、烏帽子と冠かんむりが準備できましたね。

まず、烏帽子とかんむりをそれぞれの頭の上にのりつけしましょう。

Now, you should have two sets of heads and kimonos, the Prince's hat and the Princess's crown. Let's first glue down the hat and the crown onto their heads.

ステップ 6

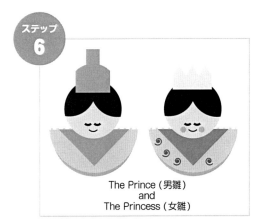

The Prince (男雛)
and
The Princess (女雛)

2人の頭をステップ④で作った着物に糊付けしたら、着物の部分をクレヨンや色鉛筆で飾ってみましょう。

In the last step, let's glue their heads onto their kimonos made in Step 4. If you like, you can further decorate their kimonos by using crayons or colored pencils.

BC

知ってると、ちょっとスマートな英語表現③

「You know what?」

直訳すると「あなたは何を知っている？」ですが、この表現は「ねぇ、知ってる？」と相手に話しかけるときに使います。

「It's news to me.」

直訳すると、「それは私にとって、ニュースです」ですが「初耳ね」という意味になります。

「It was so close!」

「close」と言うと「閉まっている」という意味を想像しますが、ここでは「近い」という意味です。

つまり、「惜しかったわ！」という意味になります。発音もクローズではなく、クロースになります。

「That's it. You've gone too far.」

That's it. は、「もうそこまで。」という表現で、You've gone too far. は「それは行き過ぎだ。」という意味です。つまり「そこまで言ったら、言い過ぎよ。」という意味になります。

「Isn't there any way?」

「なにか方法がないかしら。」という意味の表現で、「（これだけ頼んでも）どうしてもダメ？」という意味として会話に使える表現です。子どもがだだをこねたりする時も使われます。

「No means no.」

「だめなものはだめ。」という意味です。

第4章 赤ちゃんの成長 と乳児保育

Chapter 4　The Developmental Stage of an Infant and Enrolling a New Born

赤ちゃんの脳の発達には「語りかけ」が大切です。屋内でも、屋外のひなたぼっこや お散歩のときでもどんどん語りかけを行いましょう。お散歩のときに、近所の人があ やしてくれたら赤ちゃんと一緒に素敵な笑顔でお礼をいうと良いですね。今回は、赤 ちゃんの成長についての保護者との会話や赤ちゃんへの語りかけを英語で表現して みましょう。なお、本章では赤ちゃんを乳児として表記しています。

乳児（0～2ヵ月）

あら、かわいい！ひろし君の妹さんですか？かわいいですね。どれくらいですか？

8週間です！なので、もうすぐ2か月になります。

あらどうしたの？なぜ泣いてるの？

よしよし、たぶんオムツだと思います。換えなくちゃ。

どれどれ。濡れてないですよ。

じゃあ、お腹がすいたのかな。ミルクをあげないと。

あー、そのようでしたね。お腹がすいてたんですね！すごい勢いで飲んでますね！なんてかわいい赤ちゃんなんでしょ！

もうすぐ首がすわりますね、3か月くらいかな。そうしたら色々と楽になります。

Vocabulary

（生まれて）何週ですか？ How many weeks old is she?

どうしたの？ What's the matter?

よしよし There, there.

おむつ diaper

～にミルクをあげる feed ～

安定する、首がすわる be stable

Infants (0-2 months)

How cute! Is this Hiroshi-kun's baby sister? How many weeks old is she?

8 weeks! So, she is almost 2 months.

Oh, what's the matter? Why are you crying?

There, there, I think it's her diaper. Maybe I should change her.

Let's see. She's not wet.

Oh, then she must be hungry. I probably need to feed her.

Yes, that was it. She was hungry. She's drinking well! What a beautiful baby!

Soon, her neck will be stable, maybe from 3 months, which will make things easier.

出産に関係する表現
Useful Vocabulary for Pregnancy

お産する	[to] deliver a baby
妊娠する	[to be] pregnant
妊婦	[a/the] pregnant woman
つわり	[to have] morning sickness
予定日	due date
助産院	midwife clinic
助産婦	midwife
出生証明書	birth certificate

単語と英語の表現 ④

赤ちゃん（3 〜 12ヵ月）の成長の表現を 覚えましょう（要約）

3ヶ月・4カ月頃
首がすわる、声に直接反応する、笑う、刺激に反応する

5か月・6カ月頃
寝返りをうつ、喃語（なんご：ぶぅぶぅ、あーあーなど）が出る、まねる、様々な言葉の基礎づくりをはじめる、物を握る、物に手を伸ばす、離乳食を食べ始める

6か月 〜 8カ月頃
1人でお座りができる、知っている顔を認識し反応する、物に集中し、物を目で追う

9ヵ月 〜 10ヵ月頃
ハイハイができる、声の繰り返しができる、つかまり立ちができる、道具や物をうまく使える、人見知りをする

10ヵ月 〜 11ヵ月頃
簡単な言葉の意味を理解しはじめる、正しく反応できる、感情表現をする、しっかりと手の動作をする

12ヵ月頃
一人で立てる、コミュニケーションがとれる、欲しいものや欲求を表現できる、簡単な命令を理解できる、音楽にリズミカルに反応する

Important Words and Phrases ④

Milestones in the Growth of an Infant from 3-12 months （要約）

3 to 4 months
The baby's neck becomes stable (the baby's head becomes steady), reacts directly to voices, laughs and responds to stimuli.

5 to 6 months
The baby starts to roll over, begins making babbling sounds, begins to build the bases of languages, grasps and reaches for things, can begin eating solid foods.

6 to 8 months
The baby is able to sit up on her own, recognizes familiar faces and responds, focuses on things and follows them with her eyes.

9 to 10 months
The baby is able to crawl, verbally responds to prompts, is able to stand by holding something, manipulates objects, and becomes anxious around strangers.

10 to 11 months
The baby is able to understand the meaning of simple words, responds appropriately, shows clear emotional responses, clearly in control of hand movements.

1 year old
The baby is able to stand by herself, is able to communicate, express needs and desires, understands simple commands, responds rhythmically to music.

単語と英語の表現 ⑤

保育に関連する英語 ①
Useful Vocabulary When Caring for Infants ①

赤ちゃん用の
衣類洗剤と石けん
Baby laundry detergent
& Baby soap

赤ちゃんのおしりふさ
Wet ones/
Baby wipes

皮膚保護クリーム
Diaper rash cream
(eg. petroleum
jelly)

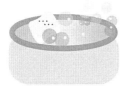

赤ちゃん用
おふろとスポンジ
Baby bath tub & sponge

コットンボールと綿棒
Cotton balls &
Cotton buds (Q-tips)

水温計
Bathwater
thermometer

おしゃぶり
Pacifier

ベビー用オイル/ローション
Baby oil/Baby lotion

おむつ替えマット
Changing mat/pad

その他

ベビーカー	Stroller	チャイルドシート	Child seat
だっこひも	Sling	搾乳器	Breast pump
		赤ちゃんのパジャマ	Sleepers/Rompers

Important Words and Phrases ⑤

保育に関連する英語 ②
Useful Vocabulary When Caring for Infants ②

よだれかけ
Bib

歩行器
Baby walker

おむつ用ゴミ箱
Odorless disposable
diaper pail

メリー/モビール
Baby mobile

ぬいぐるみ
Stuffed animal

新生児用おむつ
Diapers for
newborns

おまる
Potty

ガラガラ
Rattle

ゆりかご	Bassinet
引っかき防止用てぶくろ	Soft mittens (to prevent scratching)
ベビーベッド	Crib

BC

乳児（3か月〜5カ月）

まあ！赤ちゃんずいぶん大きくなりましたね！

おかげさまで。目で人を追うことができて、私があやすとにっこり笑ってくれてくれるんですよ。

毎日どんどん可愛くなってきます。

2人目だと、子育てにも余裕がありますか？

ええ、ひろしは1人目だったので、私たちにとってなんでも初めてで、あたふたしていましたからね。

オムツかぶれの問題などは今までありましたか？

ほとんどの赤ちゃんが困っているようですね。

幸い、使い捨ての紙オムツは以前よりずっとよくなっているので、そんなにオムツかぶれ の問題はありません。

ひろしが赤ちゃんのときは、布おむつを使っていたので、オムツが濡れると泣いて、度々オムツかぶれができていました。

そうでしたか、お2人目のお子さんはお元気そうでなによりです。

そろそろ、離乳食が始まりますよね？

そうなんです、まだおっぱいを飲んでいて、できるだけ母乳をあげたいのですが、あと1か月ぐらいで離乳食を始めようと思っています。

Vocabulary

〜をあやす play with 〜

〜にあたふたする be stressed out about 〜

オムツかぶれ diaper rash

〜に困っている be bothered by 〜

使い捨ての紙オムツ disposable diaper

布オムツ cloth diaper

以前よりずっとよくできている much better than they used to be

固形食、離乳食 solid food

おっぱいを飲む nurse

母乳 breastfeed

Infants (3-5 months)

Wow! Look at your baby girl, she has grown so much!

Yes, thank you. She can follow people with her eyes, and she smiles when I play with her.

Each day she is getting cuter and cuter.

Do you feel more relaxed with her because she is your second child?

Yes, as Hiroshi was our first child, we were stressed out about everything because it was all so new for us.

Does she ever have any problems with diaper rash?

Most babies seem to be bothered by it.

Fortunately, disposable diapers are much better than they used to be, and we haven't had many problems with diaper rash.

We used cloth diapers when Hiroshi was a baby, so he cried a lot when he wet his diaper and often had diaper rash.

I see, well it is fortunate that your second baby is doing so well.

I guess she will be eating solids soon, right?

Yes, she still nurses and I want her to breastfeed as long as possible, but I will introduce solid foods in about a month.

単語と英語の表現 ⑥

赤ちゃんの離乳食（要約）

初期：5〜6ヵ月頃

食材を基本的に噛まなくて良い状態　ピューレ状、小さじ1杯程度から

（ニンジン、リンゴ、バナナなど）

中期：7〜8ヵ月（もぐもぐ）

食材はフォークや舌でつぶせる程度の堅さ

（豆腐、アボカド、バナナなど）

後期：9〜11ヵ月（カミカミ）

前歯が生えだす時期なので、食材を歯茎でつぶせる程度の堅さ

完了期：12〜15ヵ月（パクパク）

歯も生えそろってきます。

食べ物を細かくすれば、だいたいのものが食べられます。

なお、この時期は手づかみやスプーン等で自分で食べる練習をする大切な時期です。多少散らかしたり、こぼしたりしても一人で食べさせてあげてください。

Solid Baby Foods （要約）

5 to 6 months

About 1 teaspoon of pureed foods.

(carrots, apples, bananas etc.)

6 to 8 months

Soft foods that can easily be smashed with a fork or spoon.

(tofu, avocado, banana, etc.)

10 to 11 months

Front teeth are begins to show. Solid foods the baby is able to smash with

her gums.

12 to 15 months

Almost all the teeth comes in. They can usually eat almost anything if diced

up.

Try to have them eat by themselves, by using their hands or spoons. They will

probably make a mess, but let them practice eating by themselves.

赤ちゃんの離乳食

カボチャがゆ

材　料

カボチャ（厚さ2mmの薄切り）1枚、10倍がゆ　大さじ3

作り方

① カボチャは皮を取って柔らかく茹でるか、ラップをかけて電子レンジで約30秒加熱する。

② ①をすり鉢でよくすり潰す。

③ 10倍がゆに、②を加えてよく混ぜ合わせたら出来上がりです。

肉と野菜のクリーム煮

材　料

鶏ひき肉大さじ1、カリフラワー1房、ニンジン輪切り1cm、塩大さじ1/2、ホワイトソース（豆乳で作ったもの）　大さじ1、スープ大さじ2

作り方

① ニンジンとカリフラワーを茹でてみじん切りにする。

② 鍋に①とスープを入れ、火にかける。

③ 煮立ってきたら肉を入れ、アクを取りながら柔らかくなるまで煮る。

④ 塩で薄く味付けし、ホワイトソースを加えてひと煮立ちしたら出来上がりです。

Solid Baby Food

First Stage (5-6 months)

Pumpkin Okayu

Ingredients

1 piece of pumpkin (2 mm thinly sliced pumpkin), 3 tsp. of rice porridge
* rice porridge (*okayu*) - boil rice with 10x the amount of water

How to Cook

① Boil the peeled pumpkin until soft or microwave for about 30 seconds.

② Puree the boiled pumpkin.

③ Mix the okayu and pureed pumpkin and you are ready to feed your baby.

Mid Stage (7-8 months)

Meat and Vegetable Cream Stew

Ingredients

1 tbs. ground chicken meat, 1 head of cauliflower, 1 cm sliced carrot, 1/2 tbs. salt,
1 tbs. white sauce (preferably made with soy milk), 1 tbs. soup stock

How to Cook

① Boil sliced carrot and the head of cauliflower and mince them.

② Put ① in the soup stock and turn up the heat.

③ Add ground chicken meat and skim off the soup scum or froth. Cook until the vegetables become soft.

④ Add a pinch of salt, but keep the flavor weak. Add white sauce.

BC

赤ちゃんの離乳食

野菜入り味噌おじや

材 料

軟飯子ども茶碗1/5、大根輪切り0.5ｃｍ、サトイモ１個、ネギ３ｃｍ、油揚げ1/10枚、煮干し２匹、味噌 小さじ1弱、水2/3カップ、塩少々

作り方

① 煮干でだし汁を取っておく。

② 大根は皮を剥いて柔らかく茹で、小さく切る。サトイモも皮を剥いて塩を振り、ヌメリを取って小さく切る。油揚げも小さく切り、ネギはみじん切りにする。

③ ①に軟飯と②を加えてひと煮立ちし、味噌とネギを入れて少し煮込んだら出来上がりです。

ハムと野菜のミルク煮

材 料

ハム1枚、白菜1/3枚、タマネギ1/10個、スープ1/2カップ、牛乳大さじ３、塩ひとつまみ

作り方

① ハムと野菜は１ｃｍくらいの角切りにしておく。

② 鍋に①を入れ、スープをハムと野菜がひたひたになるまで入れて煮る。

③ スープが1/3くらいになったら牛乳を加えて、再び煮込む。

④ 火を止める前に塩で薄く味をつけ、ひと煮したら出来上がり。

Solid Baby Food

Later Stage (9-11 months)

Miso Soup with Rice and Vegetables

Ingredients

1/5 cup of soft steamed rice, 0.5 cm of sliced daikon (Japanese white radish), 1 taro root, 3 cm negi (Japanese leek), 1/10 sheet of fried tofu, 2 niboshi (dried baby sardines), 1 tsp. miso, 2/3 cup water, a pinch of salt

How to Cook

① Prepare soup stock with niboshi

② Boil daikon until soft and cut into small pieces. Peel taro root and sprinkle salt on it to eliminate stickiness. Cut into small pieces. Cut fried tofu and negi into small pieces.

③ Put steamed rice in the niboshi soup, add ②, and heat. Add miso and negi and heat a little bit longer.

....

Final Stage (1 year - 1.5 years old)

Ham and Vegetable Milk Stew

Ingredients

1 slice of ham, 1/3 Chinese cabbage leaf, 1/10 onion, 1/2 cup soup stock, 3 tbs. milk, 1/16 tsp. salt

How to Cook

① Cut slice of ham and vegetables into 1 cm cubes.

② Put ① into a pan and add soup until you just cover the ham and vegetables.

③ Keep cooking until the soup is reduced by 1/3, then add milk and heat again.

④ Add salt just before you turn off the heat.

*tbs. = tablespoon; tsp. = teaspoon

乳児保育

娘をこちらの園に預けたいと思っています。何ヶ月から預かってもらえるのですか？

生後6カ月目からお預かりしています。

申し込みはいつからですか？

定員に余裕があれば、いつからでも大丈夫ですが6カ月未満はお預かりできません。6ヵ月以上の乳児は平日8時〜15時までお預かりします。

保育室を見学されますか？

ぜひ、お願いします。

お預かりするまでに、離乳食を始めておいて頂けますか？

大体何カ月目から離乳食をはじめたらよいですか？

お子様の成長によりますが、大体4〜5カ月からですね。

それから、徐々に色々な食べ物に慣らしていく場合が多いですね。

離乳食を始める前にかかりつけのお医者様にご相談してみてください。

離乳食は赤ちゃんが口にするはじめての食べ物ですから、できるだけ手作りのものをあげてください。少しの下準備で難しくありませんし、そのほうが赤ちゃんにとってもとても良いですよ。

離乳食のレシピを色々と集めて研究してみます。そうすれば健康に良い食べ物をあげはじめられますものね！

Vocabulary

〜を…に入れる enroll 〜 in...

新生児、赤ちゃん newborn/infant

申し込み手続き application process

成長 development

だいたい most likely

もう一度確認する double check

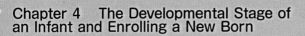

An Infant Daycare Program

I'm interested in enrolling my baby in your daycare, and I would like to know from what month you accept newborns?

We accept newborns from six months.

When can we start the application process?

If we have spaces available, anytime is fine, though we won't accept your baby until she is six months old. We offer daycare from 8 a.m. to 3 p.m. on weekdays for babies, age six months and up.

Would you like to see the newborn daycare room?

Yes, please, thank you.

Will you start feeding your baby solid food before you enroll her?

When do babies usually begin eating solid foods?

It depends on your baby's development, but most likely around four to five months and up.

Then gradually you let your baby get used to the introduction of new food into her diet.

I'd recommend that you consult with your doctor to double check that your baby is ready before starting her on solid food.

Solid food is the first real food your baby eats, so please try to give her homemade baby food. With a little advanced preparation, it really is not that hard, and it's so much better for her.

Yes, I'll try to gather different recipes and start studying, so that I can give my baby a good, healthy start!

Point 1

新生児 newborn baby

ハイハイができるくらいの赤ちゃん infant

ヨチヨチ歩きの赤ちゃん toddler

いないいないばぁ peekaboo

抱っこする hold/pick 〜 up

0歳児　保育申込書（要約）

利用規約

コースの種類

- 半日（午前9時から12時まで）
- 1日（午前9時から午後2時まで）

必要書類

- 入園願書
- 保険証
- 母子手帳
- 予防接種記録

利用上のお約束

- 保育料（入園料・保育料）のお支払いは、お子様が入園する初日までにお願いします。
- 登園・降園時間は15分単位になります。
- お休みの場合は、電話もしくはメールで必ずご連絡ください。
- お子様が病気でお休みの場合は、詳細をお知らせください。

持ち物

- オムツ（1日最低4枚）・お尻ふき・ビニール袋
- 予備の着替え（最低3セット）
- 外用の帽子・靴・衣類
- 大きなタオル2枚・小さなお手拭き1枚
- おやつと昼食（ミルク・哺乳瓶（必要に応じて最低2本））
- 水筒
- 連絡帳

※すべてのものに記名をお願いいたします。

Application Form for Infants

Terms of Enrollment

Attendance Options

- Half-day   (9:00 a.m. – 12:00 p.m.)
- Full-day   (9:00 a.m. – 2:30 p.m.)

Documentation

- Application form
- Health insurance card
- Birth record booklet (boshitechou)
- Immunization records

Policies and Reminders:

- Payment of all fees (registration and tuition) is due before the first day your child attends school.
- Tuition fees and school policies may be adjusted on a term basis.
- Please drop-off and pick-up your child within 15 minutes of the assigned times.
- Please inform the school of any absences by telephone or email.
- If you child is absent due to sickness, please inform the school of the details.

Things to Prepare

- Diapers (minimum four per day), wet wipes, plastic bags for disposal
- Extra clothing (minimum three sets)
- Headwear, footwear and clothing for outdoor play
- Two large towels, one small hand towel
- Snack and lunch (formula or milk and a minimum of two bottles, as necessary)
- Thermos (water bottle)
- Communication Notebook

※ *All items must be clearly labeled with your child's name.*

0歳児クラス　ハンドブック

登園・降園について

午前8:45-9:00の間に直接お教室までお子様をお連れください。クラス担任がお待ちしております。その際に、すべてのカバンと持ちものは、必ず直接クラス担任にお渡しください。他のお子様のものと間違えてしまったり、なくなってしまう原因となりますので、床やドアの横または廊下などに置いたままにしないようにご注意してください。

ベビーカーを園に置いて行かれる場合は、玄関左側の小さい屋根の下に置いてください。フォレガーデンプリスクールでは、如何なる紛失や破損など一切の責任を負いかねますので予めご理解をお願いいたします。

0歳児のお子様は、午後2:30-2:45の間に直接教室にお迎えにいらしてください。クラス担任が、お子様を直接引き渡し、持ちものもその際にお渡しいたします。お迎えの際にクラス担当よりその日のお子様の様子などをお伝えしますが、詳しくは、連絡帳に記載がありますので、ご確認ください。

お迎えが遅くなる場合は、できるだけほかのクラスの迷惑にならないようにお願いいたします。

登園自粛について

0歳児の免疫機能はまだ、非常に未熟です。そのため、感染症などにかかりやすく症状が悪化する場合があります。

フォレガーデンプリスクールでは、すべてのお子様が日頃から健康・安全に生活できるようガイドラインを作成しております。

お子様が、インフルエンザや溶連菌感染症などの感染する病気にかかった場合は、直ちに園にお知らせください。

感染症と診断された場合、治療後登園を再開される際、「医師の意見書」もしくは、「保護者の責任で登園届け」（感染症によって異なる）の提出をお願いしております。

発熱をした場合は、最低24時間は登園を自粛してください。

嘔吐や下痢の場合は、最低24時間は登園を自粛してください。

登園当日に、症状が良くなっていても、登園前日に、症状がみられた場合は登園を自粛してください。

Parent Handbook - Year 0 Class

Drop-off and Pick-up

Year 0 students should be brought directly to the classroom door between 8:45 and 9:00 a.m. Homeroom teachers will be waiting for them. Be sure to pass all their bags and belongings directly to the teacher. Do not leave items on the floor, by the door, or in the hallway. They can be easily missed or lost.

If you would like to leave your stroller at the school, please leave it under the small roof to the left of the main entrance. Fore Garden Preschool cannot take any responsibility for lost or damaged items.

Year 0 students should be picked up directly at the classroom door between 2:30 and 2:45 p.m. Homeroom teachers will bring the child and their belongings directly to parents at this time. They will give a small verbal report, but please check the communication notebook for more detailed information on how much they drank, slept, etc.

If you come late for drop-off, please be careful not to disturb the classes too much.

Restrictions for Attendance

Year 0 students are still building their immune systems. Contagious diseases are passed along easily and also with greater effect.

Fore Garden Preschool has created certain guidelines to help maintain the health and safety of all our students.

Please inform the school immediately if your child is infected with a contagious disease (influenza, strep throat, etc.).

Any child diagnosed with a contagious disease requires a note from a doctor to return to school.

Any child with a fever must stay home for at least 24 hours.

Any child with diarrhea or vomiting must stay home for at least 24 hours.

Do NOT bring your child to school if they had these symptoms the previous day, but seem fine in the morning.

0歳児クラス　ハンドブック

授乳について

フォレガーデンプリスクールでは、乳児に粉ミルクは与えません。

ご自宅で使用している粉ミルクを園に持参してください。鉄を多く含む製品を推奨いたします。粉ミルクは、常に多めにご持参ください。担当教師より粉ミルクの使用量や残量についてお知らせいたしますが、おうちの方にもご確認いただきますようお願いいたします。

母乳を持参希望の場合は、園に持参する24時間以降に搾乳したものを持参してください。搾乳した母乳は、飲む直前まで冷蔵保管が必要です。夏季の間や気温が高い日は、保冷剤を入れて持参してください。

哺乳瓶は最低2本持参してください。プラスチック製で必ず園から返却後は、消毒をしてください。各哺乳瓶には、必ず、お子様の名前を明記してください。

登園日設定について

0歳児のお子様は、特に保護者より申し出がない場合は、フルデイの登園日は、週3日から4日となります。また、ハーフデイの時間は、午前9:00から午後12:00となります。

登園日設定は、毎学期前にお選びいただけます。（8月、1月、4月）ただし、学期途中の変更はお受けしておりません。お仕事の予定変更などやむを得ない理由の場合は、学期の途中での変更をお受けいたします。その場合は、会社や雇用主より証明書など書類の提出をお願いしております。

屋外活動について

0歳児のお子様の屋外活動については、身体発達の観点より限られています。立つ、歩く、走る、ジャンプするなどが可能になると屋外活動をさらに楽しめるようになります。

0歳児のお子様の屋外活動に関しては、下記をご参照ください。

- お天気が良い場合は、毎日外に出かけます。その際は、人数によって、抱っこ紐やバギーを使用します。
- 夏季は、専用のビニールプールで遊びます。その際は、安全が確保されるように常に大人がお子様の様子を監視します。
- 春の根岸公園への遠足は、0歳児のお子様は全員参加となります。お天気が良ければ、芝生の上での活動が可能です。

Parent Handbook - Year 0 Class

Notes About Feeding

Fore Garden Preschool does not provide formula for infants.

Parents must select their own product and send it to school. We recommend any brand with fortified iron. Please be sure to bring some extra formula at all times. Teachers will report on formula usage and remaining amount, but it is the parents' responsibility to send in more formula when necessary.

If you wish to send in breast milk, be sure to pump it no earlier than 24 hours before bringing to school. Breast milk should be kept cool and refrigerated until the last possible moment. Please use ice packs in the summer and during hot weather seasons.

Please be sure to send in at least two bottles, which must be plastic (no glass) and sterilized each night upon return. Each bottle must be clearly labeled with the child's full name.

Limited Attendance

Year 0 students are permitted to attend full day for three or four days a week, unless requested by the parents otherwise. Half days are from 9:00 a.m. to 12:00 p.m.

Parents may choose the days of attendance at the beginning of each term (August, January, and April), but must keep that schedule until the end of the term. If a parent must make a schedule change for an unavoidable reason, such as a change in their work schedule, they may request a mid-term schedule change but must provide documented proof, such as a letter from their employer.

Outdoor Play

Outdoor play time for Year 0 students are limited due to their physical development. As children learn to stand, walk, run, and jump, they are better able to enjoy outdoor settings. However, Year 0 students will have chances to experience outdoor settings in the following ways:

- Year 0 students will be taken for walks outdoors on daily basis, as long as the weather is fine. Depending on the total number of students, they will be in a baby carrier or buggy.
- During the summer, Year 0 students will play in a special vinyl baby pool. They will be monitored carefully by an adult staff member at all times.
- Year 0 students will join all children on the spring field trip to Negishi Forest Park in Yokohama. Depending on the weather, they may be able to lie and roll in the grass during this excursion.

知ってると、ちょっと スマートな英語表現④

「I want to talk to you.」と「I need to talk to you.」

「あなたに言っておきたいことがある。」want と言う言葉は「〜がほしい」という、自分の感情を抑えられないニュアンスがあります。したがって、子どもはほとんどの場合、want を使います。I want to talk to you. といわれると、「なにかあったのか？」「悪いことしたのか？」とドキドキします。上司に言われたら深刻な話かと思ってしまいます。

「need」に置き換えると「ちょっとお話がしたいのですが。」というニュアンスになります。

「Let her have it for a while.」

おもちゃなどを取り合っているときに「しばらく彼女に貸してあげなさい。」というように使える表現です。

「Do as I say.」

「言う通りにしなさい。」

「Don't pick on her.」

「いじめないで。」

「あとはまかせて。」の色々な表現を学習しましょう。

Let me handle this.

Leave it to me.

I'll do the rest.

ABC

第5章　病気と休園
Chapter 5　　School Absence Due to Illness

虫歯の予防には歯磨きが一番です。歯を磨くだけでなく、正しい磨き方を習慣づける
ためには、先生と保護者の連携が欠かせません。また子どもはちょっとしたことで
体調をくずしたり、病気になります。園を欠席することは本人にとってもお友だちに
とっても寂しいことですが、インフルエンザ等の流行性の伝染病の場合には、園自体
も休園しなければならない事態にもなります。園児が病気になった場合の表現を学習
しましょう。

虫歯が痛みます

小野様でしょうか？フォレガーデン園の鈴木です。

はい、鈴木先生こんにちは。何かありましたか？

ひろし君が、歯が痛いと言っていて、食べたり飲んだりするのがつらそうなんです。歯医者に連れていかれた方が良いと思うのですが。

あら、たいへん。虫歯だとしたら、かなり痛いでしょうね。

ええ、かなり痛いようです。今日お昼でお水を飲んだとき、かなり痛かったようです。

それは良くないわ。近くの歯医者ですぐ診てもらえるかしら。まず予約しないといけませんね。

今日、すぐに彼を診てもらえるかわからないけど。

園から歩いてすぐの園の歯医者の先生にご連絡してみてはいかがですか？

これから予約が取れるかお電話でご確認いただけますか？

Vocabulary

どうかしましたか？ Has something happened?

〜するのがつらい have a hard time 〜 ing

虫歯 cavity

かなり痛い be in a lot of pain

すぐに right away

予約する make an appointment

A Painful Cavity

Is this Ono-san? This is Suzuki calling from Fore Garden Preschool.

Yes, hello, Suzuki-sensei. Has something happened?

Hiroshi-kun says his tooth hurts and he's having a hard time eating and drinking. Maybe you should take him to a dentist.

Oh no. If it's a cavity, it must be really painful.

Yes, he seems to be in a lot of pain. And it hurt when he drank some water during lunch today.

Oh no, that sounds bad. I wonder if the dentist near our home can see him right away. I may first need to make an appointment.

I am not sure the dentist will be able to see him today.

How about trying to contact the school dentist, who is walking distance from our preschool?

Can I ask you to call if Hiroshi can get an appointment?

子どもの診察に関連する表現
Useful Vocabulary for Children to Consult a Doctor

子どもを医者に連れていく	take a child to the doctor
診察を受ける	see / consult a doctor
救急車を呼ぶ	call an ambulance
入院する	be hospitalized
ほんのちょっとだけ副作用があります	There are only a few side effects.
お医者さんは、注射しますか？	Will the doctor give me a shot?
綿棒はありますか？	Do you have Q-Tips?

虫歯が痛みます

先生、歯が痛いよ。

どこ？どれどれ、あーんしてごらん。

あー、右の下の奥歯が虫歯になってるわね。

虫歯？だけどちゃんと歯磨いてたよ！

そうね、園でも食事の後、ちゃんと磨いていたのにね。かわいそうに。

歯医者さんに行かないとだめ？

そうね。歯医者さんに行って、早く治療してもらわないと、もっと痛くなるわよ。

痛くて、じんじんする。

お母さんに電話して、お迎えに来てもらうわ。もう少し我慢できる？

おうちで歯磨きどれくらいしている？あと、いつ歯磨きしている？

朝起きた時だよ。

一日一回では、十分じゃないわね。起きた後、食事の後それから、寝る前の1日5回は、歯磨きしたほうがいいわ。

園でお昼を食べた後の歯磨きは難しいかもしれないから、朝食と夕食の後は、必ず歯磨きをしてね、そうしたら虫歯にならないようになるからね。

A Painful Cavity

Sensei, my tooth hurts.

Where? Let me see, can you open your mouth?

Aha, you have a cavity in your bottom right tooth in the back.

A cavity? But I brush my teeth so well!

Yes, you brush your teeth well after lunch here at the preschool too. You poor thing.

Do I need to go to the dentist?

I think so. If you don't go to the dentist to have your cavity fixed, your tooth will hurt even more.

It's throbbing.

I'll call your mom and have her pick you up. Can you wait just a bit longer?

Can you tell me how many times you brush your teeth, and when do you do it every day?

I do it after I wake up.

Maybe once a day is not enough, I recommend you brush your teeth after you wake up, after each meal, and before you go to bed. That's 5 times a day.

I understand though it's difficult to brush your teeth after eating lunch at school, so make sure you brush your teeth after breakfast and dinner and try to avoid getting cavities, okay?

Vocabulary

右下の奥歯　bottom right tooth in the back

かわいそうに　You poor thing.

治療する　fix

じんじんする　throbbing

つくってみましょう ⑯ おたより編

虫歯予防教室実施の報告をしましょう（要約）

歯科教室のお知らせ

保護者各位

フォレガーデン
園長　山田　けいこ

6月7日（金）は歯科教室デーでした。園児たちも、歯のケアをすることの重要性や、虫歯予防について学びました。

地元の歯科医である　荒木　慶太先生をお招きし、歯・口・虫歯の危険性について簡単なレッスンを行いました。健康な歯と虫歯のある歯の写真を見て、子どもたちは驚いていました。

それから、先生が、液体を使って歯をチェックしました。歯垢があるところは赤くなりました。赤くなったところを見ながらじっくり歯ブラシでブラッシングを行い、きれいな白い歯になりました！

乳幼児期から歯科衛生に気を配ることが大切です。乳歯であってもしっかりと行いましょう。お子様と歯のケアについて話し合い、食後の歯磨きを心がけましょう。適切な歯磨きの習慣ができるよう、ご家庭でもお子様と一緒に心がけるようにしてください。

よろしくお願いいたします。

Let's Try ⑯

Report on Dental Care Class

Dear Parents,

Friday, June 7th was our special "Let's Take Care of our Teeth" day. All students were given the chance to learn about the importance of dental care and how to prevent cavities.

Dr. Keita Araki, a local dentist, visited the school and gave a brief lesson to the children about teeth, the human mouth, and the dangers of cavities. The children were fascinated and surprised to see pictures of healthy and unhealthy teeth.

Mr. Araki had checked students' teeth with some liquid. Areas with plague were stained red. The children then had to brush them clean with their toothbrush until all the red stains were removed, revealing clean white teeth underneath!

We'd like to remind all of you that proper dental health begins at a young age. Just because children still have their baby teeth does NOT mean that they shouldn't take care of them. Please discuss the events of this day with your child and brush with them after each meal. Please teach them to brush properly and remind them regularly.

Thank you for your understanding.

Sincerely,
Keiko Yamada, Principal
Fore Garden Preschool

単語と英語の表現 ⑦

歯にまつわるお話

日本では、乳歯（baby tooth）がぬけたら、下の歯なら屋根に、上の歯は縁の下にと、永久歯がしっかり生えるよう願いを込めて投げるという習慣がありますが、アメリカやイギリスでは、歯を枕の下におくと、歯の妖精（Tooth Fairy）が寝ている間に歯とコインを交換してくれるという言い伝えがあります

The Lovable Imaginary Tooth Fairy

Children are told that if they put a tooth that has come out under their pillow, the tooth fairy will take it away while they are sleeping and leave a coin in its place. 〔COBUILD English Dictionary〕

※イギリスには、初めて抜けた歯を、記念として残しておくための箱があって、"Tooth Fairy Box"と呼ばれています。

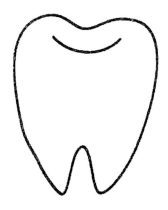

Important Words and Phrases ⑦

よく使われるけがや病状の表現
Phrases for Injuries and Illnesses

（病気に関連する表現や単語は２級テキストにも記載されていますので併せて学習してください）

のどが痛い	have a sore throat
耳が痛い	have an earache
目が痛い	have sore eyes
鼻水が出る	have a runny nose
鼻が詰まる	have a stuffy nose
鼻血が出る	have a bloody nose
しゃっくりが出る	have hiccups
くしゃみをする	sneeze
吐く	vomit / throw up
顔に引っ掻き傷をつくる	Make a scratch on the face
指をやけどする	burn one's finger
足（の骨）を折る	break one's leg
手首をひねる	sprain one's wrist
ひじを擦りむく	scrape one's elbow
詰まらせる、窒息する	choke
誤飲する	accidentally swallow/poison
しもやけになる	get frostbite

インフルエンザの流行

もしもし、小野様でしょうか？

はい、そうです。鈴木先生ですか？お元気ですか？

どうしましたか？

ありがとうございます。元気です。実は園でインフルエンザが流行っているのでご連絡しました。今日３人の園児がインフルエンザで休んでいるんですよ。

あら、それは大変ですね。

はい、そうなんです。ひろし君は大丈夫ですか？

はい、今のところは大丈夫そうです。

そうですか、よかったです。これ以上休む園児が増えるようですと、学校閉鎖をしないといけないかもしれません。ひろし君の様子も気を付けて見守ってください。

お知らせいただきましてありがとうございました。ひろしが感染しないように願っています。

Vocabulary

どうかしましたか？ Is something wrong?

インフルエンザ flu　　　　　**はやる** go around　　　　　**心配な** worrisome

学校閉鎖する cancel/close down school

〜を注意してみる keep a close eye on 〜

〜を願う keep my fingers crossed that 〜

Taking Precautions Against the Flu

Hello. Is this Ono-san?

Yes, it is. Is this Suzuki-sensei? How are you?

Is something wrong?

Thank you, I'm fine. I called to let you know that the flu seems to be going around. There were 3 kids absent from school today because of the flu.

Oh no, that's worrisome.

Yes, so I was just wondering if Hiroshi-kun is okay?

Yes, he seems okay for now.

That's good to know. If we have more kids staying home sick, then we may have to cancel school. I just wanted you to be aware and ask that you keep a close eye on Hiroshi-kun.

Thank you for letting me know. I'll keep my fingers crossed that he will be fine.

Point 1

ウイルス性疾患の名前

はしか　measles

水疱瘡　chicken pox

おたふく　mumps

風疹　rubella

インフルエンザ発生の対応についての
お知らせを作りましょう（要約）

インフルエンザ発生時の対応について

保護者各位

フォレガーデン園
園長　山田　けいこ

インフルエンザの流行期に入り、市の子ども課より保育所等の臨時休園基準についての通知がありました。市の通知に基づき、インフルエンザの感染拡大を防止するため下記の対応をおこないますので、ご理解ご協力をお願いいたします。

臨時休園の措置について

保育園で7日間連続でインフルエンザと診断された乳幼児が3人以上発生した場合、保育園は臨時休園になります。休園期間は、3人以上の発生が確認された日の翌日より5日間（土・休日含む）です。

インフルエンザを発症した園児の登園停止について

発症した翌日から7日を経過するまで登園停止とします。

登園自粛のお願い

下記のような症状、状態の場合はインフルエンザに感染していなくても登園を控えるようにして下さい。

1. 朝から37．5度以上の熱があり、元気がなく機嫌が悪いもしくは、食欲がなく朝食・水分が摂れていない場合
2. 24時間以内に解熱剤を使用している場合
3. 24時間以内に37.5度以上の熱が出ていた場合
4. 平熱より1度以上高い時（＊1歳以下の乳児の場合）
5. 37.5度以上ある時
6. 同居する家族が感染した場合（他に感染する恐れがないと医師に確認した場合は除く）

治癒後について

治癒後登園を再開される場合は、「登園証明書」の提出をお願いいたします。

Let's Try ⑰

An Outbreak of the Flu

Dear Parents,

The Flu Season is Upon Us!

In reaction to the spread of influenza (the flu), the city office has provided the following criteria to schools with regard to recommendations for closure. We appreciate your cooperation with this matter in order to limit the spread the flu virus.

Fore Garden
Principle Keiko Yamada

Measures for School Closure

If there are more than three children who are diagnosed with influenza (the flu) consecutively for seven school days in a preschool, the school is required to close temporarily. The closing term will be five days (including weekends) counted from the day after the last three children were diagnosed with the flu.

Absence of a Child

A child who is diagnosed with the flu must be absent from school for 7 days from the day after the child is diagnosed.

Terms for Self-Restraining Child from School

Please keep your child at home if a child is experiencing any of the following symptoms.

If your child:

1. Has a fever of more than 37.5 C in the morning (of a school day), is not well and feeling sick, or has no appetite, nor wants anything to drink.
2. Took antipyretic within the last 24 hours.
3. Has a fever of more than 37.5 C within the last 24 hours before going to school.
4. Has a temperature 1 degree C higher than normal (✳ If your child is younger than 1 year old).
5. Has a temperature of more than 37.5 C
6. A family member has been diagnosed with the flu (✳ unless there is doctors permission).

Procedure After Recovery

If your child has been absent because of the flu, please bring a note with your physician's signature informing the school that your child is no longer contagious.

つくってみましょう ⑱ おたより編

保健室からのお便りを作って みましょう ①（要約）

保護者各位

お知らせ

フォレガーデン園　保健室

風邪やインフルエンザが流行し、日ごと欠席者が見受けられます。

お子さんが欠席される場合、当日の朝に園に連絡をお願いします。

37．5度以上の発熱、嘔吐、激しい下痢等の症状が出た場合は自宅待機をお願いします。軽い兆候や症状であれば、園で対応します。

感染予防について

ウィルスは伝染します。食事の前とトイレのあとは手を洗い、あなた自身も周りの人も清潔を保ちましょう。消毒液を使用し、石鹸で洗った後も手に残っているバクテリアやウイルスを殺菌しましょう。お子様に下記をうながしましょう。

手を洗う前に、顔に触れるときも注意しましょう。ウイルスは口、鼻、目からも感染します。

ペットボトルや食器類を使い回さないよう気をつけてください。

マスクやハンカチで口元を覆い、感染を予防してください。

Let's Try ⑱

A Note from the School Nurse ①

Dear Parents,

With colds and the flu going around, we are seeing several absences each day.

Please remember to call the school in the morning if your child will be absent from school.

Please keep your child at home for the day if he/she has a fever over 37.5 degrees, is vomiting, or has severe diarrhea. Mild signs and symptoms can be coped with at school.

How to Avoid Seasonal Viruses:

REMEMBER ALL VIRUSES ARE CONTAGIOUS. Protect yourself and others by washing your hands before eating and after going to the bathroom. When possible, please use a sterilizing gel to kill any bacteria and viruses that might remain after washing your hands with soap.

Please remind your child (ren) of the following points:

DO NOT TOUCH YOUR FACE before washing your hands. Germs enter our bodies through the MOUTH, NOSE, AND EYES.

DO NOT SHARE water bottles or other drinking and eating utensils.

COVER YOUR COUGH with a mask or handkerchief.

Sincerely,
School Nurse

保健室からのお便りを作ってみましょう ② (要約)

出席停止・伝染病の扱いについて

伝染病に罹患またはその疑いがある、もしくはかかるおそれのある園児は、基準に基づき、欠席扱いとはなりませんのでゆっくりと静養させ、完全に治癒させてから登園させてください。

出席停止扱いとなる伝染病

はしか・百日咳・流行性結膜炎・風疹・とびひ・おたふく風邪・手足口病・インフルエンザ・コレラ・赤痢・腸チフス・しょうこう熱・結核・流行性脳髄膜炎・ジフテリア・日本脳炎・上記以外の伝染病

園児は下記症状への回復が確認できるまで自宅療養してください。

水疱瘡	全ての疱疹がかさぶたになる
風疹	発疹が消える
麻疹	熱が収まってから三日の経過
おたふく風邪	腫れがひく
百日咳	咳がおさまる
喉頭炎	医者の了承
伝染性の目の病気	医者の診断書が必要

ABC

Let's Try ⑲

A Note from the School Nurse ②

How to Deal with Contagious Illnesses

If your child has a contagious illness, his or her absence will not count as an absence, based on certain school protocol. Please have your child rest and only send him or her back to school after the conditions listed below are met.

Most Common Contagious Illnesses:

Measles, Whooping Cough, Infectious Eye Diseases, German Measles, Impetigo, Mumps, Hand, Foot, and Mouth Disease, Flu, Cholera, Dysentery, Typhoid Fever, Scarlet Fever, Tuberculosis, Cerebrospinal Fever, Diphtheria, Japanese Encephalitis etc.

Students are required to remain at home until the following conditions are observable:

Chicken Pox	:	All blisters have become dry scabs.
German Measles	:	Rash has disappeared.
Measles	:	Three days with no fever.
Mumps	:	The swelling subsides.
Whooping Cough	:	The cough ceases.
Strep Throat	:	On doctor's recommendation.
Infectious Eye Diseases	:	A doctor's form is required.

臨時休園のお知らせ（電話連絡網）

- もしもし、フォレガーデン園の荒木たえこの父ですが。

- おはようございます。どうしましたか？

- 園から連絡事項があります。インフルエンザのため、今日は休園するそうです。

- 今年のインフルエンザは猛威をふるっていますね。私の知っている人は皆、インフルエンザにかかっているか、身近な人がかかっているかですよ。

- 他の園でも休園にしているところが多くあるそうですよ。うちの園ではインフルエンザで自宅にいる子どもたちはそれほどいないみたいですけどね。フォレガーデンは、毎日ラジオ体操をかかさないからですかね。

  まあ、何にせよ、それ程多くなくてよかったですよね。

  次の方に連絡網を回して頂けますか？

  モハメド君のママは、日本語は大丈夫ですか？

- 確かではありませんが、この連絡事項を伝えるくらいであれば、私の英語力でも大丈夫だと思います。

  もし、わからないようであれば、後ほどメールをしておきます。メールアドレスを知っているので。

- 良かったです。よろしくお願いします。早くインフルエンザの流行時期が終わるといいですね。お体に気をつけてください。

Vocabulary

〜を…に回す pass 〜 on to …

…出来るほど〜 〜 enough to …

School Closing

Hello. This is Taeko Araki's father, from Fore Garden Preschool.

Good morning. Is there anything wrong?

I have some information from school. The school will be closed today due to the flu.

The flu this year is really going around. It seems everyone I know either has it or knows someone who has it.

I heard many other schools are already closed. It seems that we don't have as many children at home with the flu at our school. I wonder if it is because Fore Garden makes the children do Radio Taiso exercises every day.

Well, whatever the reason, I am glad for it.

Can you please pass the message on to the next person on the phone tree?

Does Mohammed's mom speak Japanese?

I'm not sure, but I think my English is good enough to give her this message.

If she doesn't understand the message, then I will send her an email. I know her email address.

Oh, good. Thank you. I hope the flu season will soon be over. Please take care and try to stay well.

Point 1

It seems everyone I know either has it or knows someone who has it.

この文の主節は It seems で、仮主語 it の意味上の主語が that 以下です。that 節内は、everyone I know を主語にとる動詞が has と knows の二つで、それを either … or ～が修飾しています。つまり、「私の知っている人は皆、インフルエンザにかかっているか、かかっている人を知っているかのどちらかだ。」が直訳の意味です。

知ってると、ちょっとスマートな英語表現 ⑤

「We might as well.」

なにかの相談をしている際に「そうするしかないわね。」という意味で使う表現です。

「It could have been a lot worse.」

「状況がもっと悪くなってもおかしくなかった」の意味で、「せめてもの救いだわ。」という表現です。

「Am I making sense?」

「私の言っていることはきちんと意味がとおっている？」という意味になります。

独り言でつぶやくときにも使います。

「It's not nice to talk back to me like that.」

「talk back」は口答えの意味で、「そのような口答えはよくない。」という意味になります。

「What a day!」

「なんという日でしょう！」という意味の表現です。どちらかというと悪い場合に使われることが多いようです。

「すごくいい日だった！」という時は「What a nice day!」となります。

「最悪の日だった！」という場合「What a terrible day!」となります。

「Are you on the tall side?」

直訳すると「あなたは、背が高い側ですか？」です。つまり「背は高いほうですか?」の意味になります。

第6章　緊急時対応の訓練
Chapter 6　　　An Emergency Drill

楽しい行事の会話を練習しましょう

大地震を経験して、多くの教育関係者が引取訓練や避難訓練の重要性を再認識しました。お預かりしている園児の安全を確保するため、これまで以上に真剣かつ慎重な訓練を心掛けましょう。災害時の会話を表現してみましょう。

引き取り訓練の連絡

来週の火曜日は、園児の引き取り訓練をおこないますので、よろしくお願いします。

そうでした。火曜日の11時でしたね？保護者は徒歩か自転車で子どもを引き取りにくるように連絡帳に書いてありました。そうでしたよね？

はい、災害時は、車や電車等の交通機関が乱れるおそれがあります。引き取りに自宅から徒歩か自転車でどのくらいかかるか、前もって予想していただければと思います。

遠くから通園しているご家族は大変ですね。

そうなんです。保護者が遠方にお住まいだったり、勤め先から園まで来られないことがあります。その場合、保護者の方がお迎えにいらっしゃれるまで、園でお預かりすることになります。

その訓練も兼ねているんですよ。当日は、引き取りカードを必ずお持ちくださいね。

はい、わかりました。 ではその時に。

Vocabulary

緊急事態 emergency

訓練 drill

〜と書いてある it is indicated that 〜

〜という可能性が高い
there is a high possibility that 〜

公共交通機関 public transportation

応じて accordingly

Emergency Pick-Up Drill and Information

Please don't forget that we have an emergency pick-up drill next Tuesday.

That's right. It's at 11 a.m. on Tuesday, right? It was indicated in the communication booklet that parents have to pick-up their child either by walking or bike. Is this right?

Yes, during an emergency there is a high possibility that cars and public transportation will be running irregularly. We would like you to know how long it'll take you to come to pick up your child by walking or by bike, so you can plan accordingly.

That'll be hard for some families coming to school from far away.

Yes. For those families living or working some distance from school, they may not be able to pick their child or children up. In this case, the school will let those children stay at the school until their parents can make it to pick them up.

We would like to practice this, too. Please don't forget to bring the emergency ID card with you when you come in on Tuesday.

Okay. I'll see you, then.

Point 1

Please don't forget to bring the emergency ID card with you …

bring はこの語だけで「～を持ってくる」の意味が成り立ちますが、with 人をつけることで「あなた本人が～を持ってくる」と、本人が来ることを強調しています。

つくってみましょう ⑳ おたより編

緊急連絡訓練（引き取り訓練）の お知らせ（要約）

緊急連絡訓練（引き取り訓練）のお知らせ

保護者各位

フォレガーデン園
園長　山田　けいこ

５月25日（水）・26日（木）に緊急連絡訓練（引き取り訓練）を予定しています。
この訓練は保育中の時間帯に緊急事態が発生したという想定で行われます。

この訓練の目的は：

① 非常時に保護者と緊急連絡を取ること

② 安全にすべての子ども達を保護者に引き渡すこと

この訓練を通して効果的な安全対策を目指し、お子様を安全に引き渡したい
と思いますので、皆様のご協力をよろしくお願いいたします。

実施内容：訓練は２つのパートに分けて行います

1. 連絡方法

保育、授業時間中に、一斉電話連絡システムを使って皆さんに連絡を流しま
す。連絡が入ったら、速やかにお迎えにきてください。
緊急時は交通手段が使用できないもしくは制限されることがあり、これを前
提にした訓練ですので、趣旨をご理解いただき、お手数でも徒歩でのお迎え
をお願いします。

2. 引き取り方法

お子様をお引き取りの際には、引き取りカードを必ず持参してください。
引き取りカードがない場合、お引き取りができないことがあります。

Emergency Pick-Up Drill

Emergency Pick-Up Drill

Dear Parents,

We are planning have an Emergency Pick-Up Drill on Wednesday, May 25 and Thursday, May 26. This procedure is set to occur in the event of an emergency while the children are at school.

The purpose of this drill is to:

① To practice contacting parents during an emergency

② To practice returning all children to their parents safely

It is our intention that in the event of an emergency, we will have an effective and safe system in place to return all children to their parents safely. We appreciate your cooperation.

Sincerely,
Principal Keiko Yamada

Plan for the Drill: We have two different drills planned.

1. Procedures for Making Contact:

We will call you through the emergency telephone contact system during school hours. As soon as you receive a call, please come to pick-up your child.
Please understand that this is an emergency drill, so please come and pick your child up on foot or by bike, even though it may be a hassle. There is a high possibility that in the event of an actual emergency, public transportation will be running irregularly, so we request that you do not drive to pick-up your child.

2. Procedure for Pick-Up:

Please make sure you have your emergency ID card with you when you come and pick your child up. We may not be able to release the child to you if you don't have your emergency ID card with you.

BC

引き取り訓練

只今から引き取り訓練を行います。

園児は園庭でクラスごとに並んで座っています。

保護者の方は、園庭に行き、お子様を引き取ってください。

小野ひろしの保護者です。ひろしを引き取りに来ました。

引き取りカードをご提示ください。

はい、これです。

ありがとうございます。引き取りカードの記載内容を照合します。お名前とご住所と園児とのご関係を教えてください。

あら、結構大変な手続きをおこなうんですね。

はい、実際の災害時はかなりの混乱が予想され、引き渡す担当もクラスの担任とは限りませんから、間違いのないように訓練を実施しております。

そうですね。ありがとうございます。様々なことを想定して考え頂いていることがわかり、安心です。

Vocabulary

引き取り訓練 a pick-up drill

手続き procedure

〜を担当する be in charge of 〜

〜して安心する it is a relief to 〜

Emergency Pick-Up Drill

Everyone, we are about to start our emergency pick-up drill.

All the children are sitting down on the playground in lines per class.

Parents, please go to the playground to pick up your children.

I'm Hiroshi Ono's mom. I came to pick up Hiroshi.

Please show me your emergency ID card.

Here it is.

Thank you. Let me double check whether all the indicated information here is alright. Could you please tell me your name, address, and your relationship to the child?

Wow, this is quite a process.

Yes, we would like to practice this procedure very carefully because the homeroom teachers may not be in charge of this procedure in the event of an actual disaster considering all of the confusion at such a time.

Oh, I see. Thank you for organizing this. It is a relief to know that you have all thought about this so carefully.

Point 1

Wow, this is quite a process.

quite は副詞として、「完全に、まったく、すっかり」の意味で動詞や形容詞を修飾しますが、ここでは＜ quite ＋冠詞＋名詞＞で「かなりの」と言う意味になります。such なども We had such a wonderful time. のように、同様の使い方をします。

引き取り訓練

今日は、みんなで災害が起きた場合の引き取り訓練をします。

引き取り訓練は、将来起こるかもしれない色々な自然災害に備えて安全におうちの方に皆さんを迎えに来てもらう訓練です。

面白いの？

あら、ひろしくん。今はそんな風に考えていたらだめですよ。

引き取り訓練は、とても大切なんですよ。

先日、とても大きな地震があったでしょ？あのときも前もって訓練をしていたから、すべてがスムーズにできて、全員が無事だったのよ。

ごめんなさい。

どれだけ大切かが、分かってくれたらいいわ。

もうすぐ園内放送で、避難訓練の指示があります。

放送が聞こえたら、この防災ずきんをかぶって、廊下に2列にならんでください。

出る前に、防災ずきんをかぶる練習をしましょうね。

Vocabulary

順調に進む go smoothly

防災ずきん an emergency cushion

出る head out

Emergency Pick-Up Drill

 Today, we are going to practice an emergency pick-up drill.

This drill is organized to practice the procedure that we have in place so that all of you will be safely picked up by your parents in the event of any possible natural disaster that could happen in the future.

Is this going to be fun?

Oh, Hiroshi-kun. This is not a time to think like that.

This drill is important.

We had a big earthquake the other day, right? Because we practiced beforehand, everything went smoothly and all of the children in the school were safe.

I'm sorry.

As long as you understand how important this is, then it's alright.

Okay now, soon, you'll hear the school announcement starting the drill.

Once you hear the announcement, put your emergency cushion on your head and line up in twos in the hallway.

Before we head out, let's practice how to put the emergency cushion on your head.

Point 1

避難訓練

日本は世界有数の地震大国で、小さい頃から学校などで地震の避難訓練（earthquake drill）や火事を想定した避難訓練（fire drill）を行いますが、国によっては竜巻の避難訓練(tornado drill)などを行う地域もあります。加えて、近年多発している銃撃事件を受けて、襲撃や不審者から身を守る訓練（lockdown drill）など、人災を想定した訓練を実施せざるを得ない地域もあります。

つくってみましょう ㉑ 工作編

防災ずきんの作り方 (要約)

防災ずきんには様々な作り方があり、書店やインターネット等で資料は簡単に見つけられますので参考にしてください。ここでは、作り方の英文例を紹介する目的ですので、簡略記載となっています。

防災ずきんとは

中に綿やその他の緩衝用素材をいれた布製の袋で、非常時に頭にかぶり使用します。

材料	不燃性布地	横60cm×縦90cm（大きさは目安です。お子様の頭のサイズを測ってきめてください。）
	中綿	横30cm×縦80cm
	マジックテープ	1本(あごで留めるベルトとして使用します。)

ステップ 1

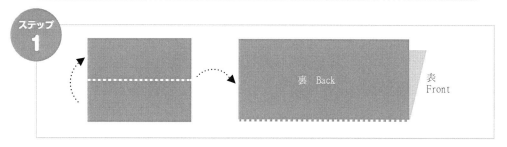

裏地面を表側にして二つに折り、重なった左右を縫い付けて袋状にします。

Fold the piece of fabric in half. Make sure the fabric is placed together front-to-front（you should be working with the fabric inside-out）. Then, sew both sides together to make it look like a bag.

ステップ 2

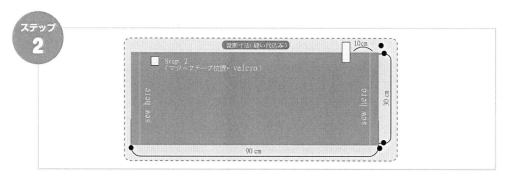

縫い付けていない開いた面の左右の端にマジックテープがくっつくように縫い付けます。（マジックテープは、あごの下で留めるベルトになります。）

Attach one side of the Velcro to the right side and then attach it to the other side, as shown in the picture 2（this becomes the Velcro band that straps across your chin）.

How to Make an Emergency Cushion

There are several ways to make an emergency cushion, and you can find more about how to make these protective cushions at bookstores and on the internet. Here we show a simple way to make an emergency cushion in order to introduce this simple sewing activity in English.

What is an Emergency Cushion?

It is a cushion made with quilted fabric that is stuffed with soft, cotton fiber that you wear on your head during emergencies.

Materials		
	Inflammable fabric	60cm × 90cm *these are the general measurements, please measure your child's head for exact measurements.
	Soft filling	30cm × 80cm
	Velcro	1 strip (this becomes a band to hold your child's chin)

ステップ 3

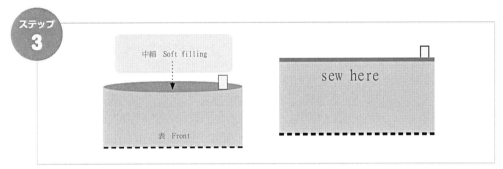

袋を裏返しにして、表地を表にします。用意した綿を袋にまんべんなく入れ、開いていた辺を縫い付けます。

Turn the fabric inside-out (you want the front of the fabric on the outside). Fill the cushion with the soft cotton fiber and spread it out so that it is flat. Sew up the open side of the fabric. (see picture 3)

ステップ 4

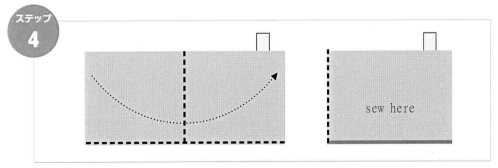

長辺を二つに折って、マジックテープの縫い付けていない方の辺を縫い付けます。

Fold in half again and sew the side where the Velcro straps are not attached, so that the cushion will fit onto your child's head.

B C

避難訓練

明日10時から避難訓練を行います。 今回は、地震を想定した避難訓練です。

東日本大震災でも、日頃の避難訓練が多くの園児の命を救ったと言われています。

この訓練では、10時に地震発生のアナウンスを流します。

アナウンスが聞こえたら、直ちに園児に防災ずきんをかぶせて机の下にもぐらせてください。3分後に、「揺れが収まったので園庭に避難してください。十分に安全だとわかったら、区より指定されている避難場所の有栖川山公園へ避難を始めてください」とアナウンスを流します。園児を廊下に2列に並べて静かに速やかに園庭に移動してください。

今日、ひろし君は足をくじいて歩くことができません。訓練中、教室で待機させてもよろしいですか?

災害発生の時に園児が歩けないこともありえますので、そのような場合のためにもこれはよい訓練の機会です。彼を車いすに乗せて同行してください。

なお、乳児担当の先生方は、乳児をベビーカーに乗せ、先生方は子どもを1名ずつおぶって避難してください。

いずれの先生方も、緊急事態においても協力し合って、自分の担当しているクラスだけではなく、園児全員の動きに目をくばらないといけません。避難訓練においても実際の緊急事態においても、それぞれが子どもたちの動きに目をくばってください。

Vocabulary

避難訓練 an evacuation drill

避難する evacuate

はう crawl

指示 instructions

避難場所 evacuation site

車いす a wheelchair

ベビーカー a stroller

〜しなければならない it is imperative that 〜

位置 whereabout

Evacuation Drill

We are going to have an evacuation drill from 10 a.m. tomorrow. This time, we are preparing for an earthquake drill.

We heard that these daily practices saved many children's lives when the Higashi Nihon Earthquake happened.

For this practice, we will announce that an earthquake has happened at 10 a.m.

As soon as you hear the announcement, please have the children put their emergency cushions on their heads and have them crawl under their desks. Three minutes later, we will announce the following, "The shaking has stopped, so head out to the playground. When it is safe enough, we will make our way to Arisugawayama Park, which is our designated evacuation site." Now, let's have the children line up in twos in the hallway and start moving out to the playground as quickly and smoothly as possible.

Hiroshi-kun can't walk today because he twisted his leg. Can I have him stay in the classroom during the drill?

There might be a case like this where a student may not be able to walk by him/herself during an emergency, so this is a good opportunity to practice for such a possibility. Please have him ride in a wheelchair.

For teachers in the infant daycare, put the babies in strollers and have each teacher carry one baby on her back, please.

It is imperative that all teachers cooperate during an emergency by keeping all eyes and ears on all children in our care, not just your own group. Please help each other and be aware of all children's movements and whereabouts during both the drill and in the event of an actual emergency.

Point 1

2008年にアメリカで始まった「ShakeOut」という地震防災訓練では、「Drop（まず低く）, Cover（頭を守り）, Hold on（動かない）」を標語としています。

避難訓練

今日は、避難訓練を行います。

避難訓練というのは、地震や火事が起きた時のための練習です。

ケガすることなくみんなが避難できるようにしなければいけません。

前もって訓練することは大切ですから、今日はみんな頑張ってくださいね。

どうやってやるの？

「地震です！」というアナウンスが流れたら、先生が「机の下にもぐってください」といいます。

そうしたら、机の後ろにかかっている防災頭巾を頭にかぶって、机の下にもぐってね？

先生の指示に従ってくださいね？

十分安全になったら、みんなで園庭に出て、有栖川山公園に避難します。今日はお庭に行くときに靴を履き替える必要はありません。それから、おしゃべりはしないでください、わかりましたか？

地震って、グラグラするんでしょ？怖くないの？

今回は訓練ですからね、地面は揺れはないから心配しないで。

でも、訓練をちゃんとやらないと、避難する時にケガをしたりするかもしれないでしょ？

だから、今日は真剣にやってね、わかった？

Evacuation Drill

 Today, we are going to have an emergency drill.

An evacuation drill is practice to prepare for when a big earthquake or fire might happen.

We need to make sure that we can evacuate children safely without getting injured.

It is important that we practice these procedures ahead of time, so do the best that you can do today.

 How are we going to do this?

 As soon as we hear the announcement, "It's an earthquake!", I will tell you all, "crawl under your desks".

The first thing you need to do is to put your emergency cushion on your head — it is hanging behind your desk — and then crawl under the desk, okay?

It is important to follow my instructions, okay?

Once it is safe enough, we will go out to the playground and evacuate to Arisugawayama Park. You do not have to change your shoes when you go to the playground today. Also, there will be no talking, okay?

 The earthquake will cause a lot of shaking, right? Isn't it scary?

This is a drill, so the ground will not shake, so don't worry.

But, if you don't practice the drill properly, you may get injured during the evacuation, right?

Please take the practice today seriously, okay?

Vocabulary

避難する evacuate

ちゃんと練習する practice the drill properly

原因となる cause

真剣に seriously

つくってみましょう ㉒ おたより編

地震の発生の場合の対応について（例）（要約）

●登園前、登園途中、降園途中、および帰宅後に大規模地震判定会招集や大規模地震警戒宣言発令、大規模地震が発生した場合

→ 保護者のご判断のもとに避難行動をとってください。

●保育中に大規模地震判定会が招集された時、大規模地震警戒宣言が発令された時、大きな地震（震度5以上）が発生した時

→ 直ちに園にお子様のお引き取りをお願いします。交通機関の麻痺等で、速やかなお引き取りが困難と思われる場合は園への連絡を試みてください。交通機関が回復した際には、できる限り早く、かつ安全な方法で、園に向かってください。お引き取りに来られるまでお子様は園が責任をもってお預かりします。必ず引き取りカードをご持参ください。

●保育中に、震度4以下の地震の場合

→ 園の判断により、お子様のお引き取りをしていただく場合があります。その場合、電話連絡網およびメールにより引取りの連絡をいたしますので、連絡を受けたら、お子様をただちにお引き取りに来てください。必ず引き取りカードをご持参ください。

ABC

Sample Regulations
What to Do When an Earthquake Strikes

● During an impending disaster or hazardous situation, such as when a big earthquake strikes before going to school, on the way to school, or on the way back home from school, all children should:

→ Please take evacuation action at the discretion of the guardian.

● When an emergency occurs while the children are at school, such as 5 + earthquake on the earthquake scale, please do the following:

→ Pick your child up from school immediately. If public transportation is not running regularly, try to contact the school and let us know that you are having difficulty getting to school to pick up your child. As soon as the transportation system is back up and running, please get to the school using the safest way possible and pick up your child as quickly as possible. The school will keep your child safely at school until you are able to come and pick him or her up. Please do not forget your emergency ID card.

● When an earthquake of 4 or lower strikes while children are at school:

→ Based on the school's decision, you may be asked to pick up your child. In this case, the school will contact you using the telephone tree and/or email. Upon receiving the call, please come and pick up your child as soon as possible. Please do not forget your emergency ID card.

BC

単語と英語の表現 ⑧

非常用持ち出しセットの例	Sample List of Emergency Supplies
① 飲料水運搬バケツ 4 L	① Bucket for drinking water（4 liters）
② 缶入カンパン（110 g × 2 缶）	② Canned crackers（2 cans x 110 g）
③ 缶入り飲料水（425ml × 2 缶）	③ Canned drinking water（2 cans x 425 ml）
④ 懐中電灯（予備電池付き）	④ Flashlight（with spare batteries）
⑤ 非常用ローソク（マッチ付き）	⑤ Candles（with a lighter or matches）
⑥ 万能シート（1800mm × 1800mm）	⑥ Multi-purpose vinyl sheet（1,800 mm x 1,800 mm）
⑦ クイックコンロ（携帯袋・燃料付き）	⑦ Portable gas cooking stove（portable bag with spare gas cylinders）
⑧ アルミ箔ナベ（3 個）	⑧ Aluminum pan（3）
⑨ 3 人用食器セット	⑨ Dishes for 3 people
⑩ ロープ（5 m）	⑩ Rope（5M）
⑪ 救急セット	⑪ First Aid Kit
内容　三角巾、ガーゼ、油紙（2枚）、伸縮包帯（2個）、脱脂綿、救急絆創膏（10枚）、紙絆創膏、綿棒（10本）、ハサミ、とげ抜き兼用ピンセット	Others　Triangular bandages, Gauze, Oil sheet（2）, Bandages（2 rolls）, Cotton balls, Adhesive bandage,（10）, Paper band-aid, Cotton Swab（10）, Scissors, Tweezers

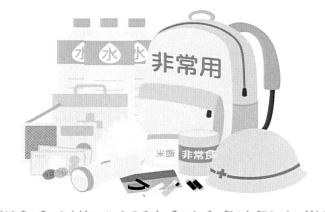

第7章　就学前の教育
Chapter 7　Education Prior to Enrollment

就学前園児により教育的な要素が取り入れられてきています。園児の学習意欲や習い事のニーズの高まりに応えていくのも大切です。習い事に関する会話を学びましょう。

話を聞いて、思い浮かんだシーンを描いてみましょう

今から、先生がお話を読みます。頭の中に浮かんだことを画用紙に描いてみましょう。お話は、とても簡単な内容です。

たろう君の日曜日　　　　作：梶原　諭

今日は、日曜日。たろう君が、楽しみにしていたパパと遊園地に行く日だよ。

外で待っていたパパが、たろう君に「早くおいで〜。出発するよー」

と声をかけながらブッブッと鳴らしました。

「ブッブーー」て、何の音？そう。車のクラクションだね。

ということは、たろう君は、どうやって、遊園地に行くのかな？

そう。車で行くんだね。

たろう君のうちの車は何色だろうね？

今日は、すごく晴れているの。晴れているから、空は何色？そう。青空だね。

遊園地についたたろう君は、とてもうれしくてたまりません。チャラン、チャラン

あれ、これは何の乗り物？

遊園地に行くとみんなのりたくなる乗り物だよ。

そう、メリーゴーラウンドの音だね。

メリーゴーラウンドにはどんな乗り物があるかな？

そう、お馬さんがあるね。馬車もあるね。

兵隊さんが行進しているよね。カボチャの馬車もあるよね。

女王様もいるし、楽しいよねー。

パパと遊園地で楽しい一日を過ごしたたろう君は、お家に帰りました。

ピンポーン。

あれ何の音？そうだね。

玄関のチャイムをたろう君が押したんだね。

そして、家で待っていたママに、なんと言ったのかな？

そう「ただいま！」って言ったんだね。

そしたら、ママは、なんと言ってくれたかな？

そう、「お帰りなさい」と言ってくれたんだね。

Listen to a Story and Visualize

 I am going to read a story to you now. I want you to draw what you visualized from the story on some blank paper.

Taro's Sunday

Today is Sunday. It's the day that Taro has been waiting for to go to the amusement park with his dad.

Dad, waiting for Taro outside, was calling to Taro, "Come on. We are leaving soon!"

Beep, beep! What's that sound?   Yes, it's the car horn.

So, how will Taro go to the amusement park?

Yes, he is going by car.

I wonder what color the Taro's family car is.

We have a clear, sunny day today.

What would the color of the sky be, then? Yeah, blue!

As Taro arrived at the park, he couldn't hold in his excitement. He wanted to ride the attractions as soon as possible. Jingle, jingle!

Wait, what is this ride?

It is the one that everyone wants to ride in at the amusement park.

Yes, that is the sound of a merry-go-round.

What kind of rides does a merry-go-round have?

Yes, there are horses. Yes, there are horse carriages as well.

There's a float with lights on it.

There are some soldiers marching. There's also a pumpkin horse carriage.

There's even a queen marching. It's fun!

After spending a great day with his dad, Taro went back home.

Ding, dong!

Hey, what's that sound?

Yes, Taro pressed the doorbell.

And what do you think Taro said to his mom, waiting for him at home?

Yes, he said, "I'm home!"

And then what did his mom say?

Yes, she said, "Welcome back home!"

話を聞いて、思い浮かんだシーンを描いてみましょう

 今、先生が読んだお話で、自分が思い浮かんだ場面を絵にしてみましょうね。

まず、思い浮かんだことを鉛筆で薄く画用紙に描いてみてくださいね。

例えば、たろう君がお父さんの運転する車に乗ろうとしているところが頭に浮かんで、絵にしようとしますね。どんな色の車？大きい？小さい？

画用紙いっぱいに車を描いてしまったら、たろう君が乗れませんね。

お父さんはどんな顔でたろう君を待っていますか。

どんな顔のお父さんを思い浮かべましたか？

メガネはかけていましたか？太っていましたか？

着ていた服の色は？

たろう君は帽子をかぶっていますか？水筒は持っていますか？

お話を聞き逃した人もいるかもしれませんね。もう一回読みますよ。

頭の中に思い浮かんだことはすぐに変わっていきますから今度読んだら、先生は、なにも話しません。すぐに画用紙に思い浮かんだ場面を鉛筆で薄く描いてください。何を描くか決まったら、絵の具を使ってください。

同じ話を聞いても、隣の人と同じところが思い浮かんだり、同じ色になったりはしないでしょう。

上手も下手もありません。それでいいのです。

一人一人が、お話を聴いて頭に浮かんだイメージを絵にするということが大切です。

はい、ではもう一度読みます。

Listen to a Story and Visualize

 Based on the story that I just read to you, I want you to draw a picture of what you've imagined.

We will be using paints, but it may be challenging to imagine if you paint straight away, so draw what you have imagined lightly using your pencil at first.

For example, if you imagine the scene when Taro is about to get in Dad's car and draw it, what's the color of the car? Is it big or small?

If you draw the car so that it fills up the paper, you won't be able to draw Taro getting into the car.

Also, you should think about how his dad looked when he was waiting for Taro.

What do you imagine his dad looks like?

Does he wear glasses? Is he big?

What color of clothes does he wear?

Does Taro wear a cap? Does he carry a water bottle?

Perhaps some of you have missed some details of my story, so let me read it once again.

Things that come into your mind can change quickly, so this time I'll be silent as I finish reading the story. I then want you to sketch on the paper what you came up with straight away. Once you are sure about what to draw, then you can start using the paint.

Even when we hear the same story, you will not imagine the same thing as your neighbors or even have the same color combinations as others.

There aren't good or bad drawers. Anything is alright.

It is important to draw pictures that each one of you imagined.

Okay, I am going to read it again now.

 Point 1

お絵かきに関することば

drawing　お絵かき	doodle　ノートなどにする落書き
scribble　ぞんざいに書いた落書き	sketch　写生　　graffiti　壁に書かれた落書き

文字を教えます

 今日は、ひらがなのお勉強をしましょう。

私たちが話している言葉は、日本語といいます。ほかの国の人たちは別の言葉で話します。例えば、中国の人は中国語を話し、アメリカの人は英語、フランスの人はフランス語を話します。

その言葉には、本を読んだり、手紙を書いたり出来るように、文字があります。私たちが使っている日本語には、ひらがなとカタカナと漢字という3種類の文字があります。

教室の前の壁に、50音ひらがなカタカナ表が貼ってありますね。

ひらがなとカタカナは、文字としては違いますが、同じ発音です。

右端の一番上にある文字は、ひらがなでは「あ」、カタカナでは「ア」と書いてありますが、どちらも「a」という発音です。

ですから、ひらがな表で順番に発音を覚えると、カタカナ表も簡単に覚えることができます。

皆さん、先生が、"あいうえお" を、ゆっくりと発音しますから先生の口をしっかり見ていてください。発音するときに、口の形が違います。

「あ・い・う・え・お」。わかりますね。では、先生の口の形を見ながら、発音してみましょう。準備はいいですか。大きな声で、一緒に始めますよ。

Basic Writing

 Today we're going to learn about Hiragana characters.

The language we are speaking and listening to is called Japanese. People in other countries speak different languages, as we know. For example, people in China speak Chinese, Americans speak English, and French speak French.

They also have characters they use to read books and to write letters in their languages. In our language, Japanese, we have three types of characters. They are hiragana, katakana, and Chinese characters called kanji.

You see the 50-character hiragana and katakana charts on the front of the classroom, right?

Hiragana and katakana are different characters, but they are pronounced the same.

The character at the top right corner in the hiragana chart is written あ, and on the katakana chart it's written ア, but both are pronounced "a".

This means that if we remember how to pronounce all the words in hiragana in order, you can memorize the katakana chart easily as well.

Listen, I'm going to slowly pronounce あ, い, う, え, お (a, i, u, e, o) so please watch my mouth carefully. The shape of my mouth is different when I pronounce each one.

あ, い, う, え, お. You see? Let's now pronounce them together, watch the shape of my mouth. Okay, ready? Together in a loud voice.

Point 1

文字と発音に関する言葉を覚えましょう

文字 letters　　　　発音 pronunciation　　　　母音 vowel　　　　子音 consonant

濁音 a voiced consonant　　　　　　　　半濁音 a p-sound in the kana syllabary

文字を教えます

今日は、ひらがなのお勉強をします。

ひらがなを覚えると、自分で絵本が読めるようになってすごく楽しいですよ。がんばりましょうね、いいかな。

このカードの色は何色ですか？

あお色です。

正解です。はい、カードを裏返すと文字が書いてありますね。見てわかるように、「あお」はひらがなでこのように書きます。

今日は「あお」の「あ」をお勉強します。

はい、みなさん、人差し指を出してください。いいですか？

まず、右に向かって書きます。止めます。

それから、上から下にまっすぐ下げてとめます。

次に、右の上の方から斜め下に指をおろしてそれから大きなカーブを描きます。

はい、それではもう一度、やってみましょう。

できましたか？

では、みんなの机の上にある紙に練習してみましょう。

できました！

ひろし君、よくできてるわ。家に帰ってからも練習してみてね。次に「あお」の「お」の練習をしましょう。

Vocabulary

親指　〈手の〉a thumb；〈足の〉a big toe

人差し指　the forefinger; the index finger; the first finger

中指　middle finger; second finger

薬指　the third finger; the ring finger　（主に左手の）

小指　〈手の〉the little finger；〈足の〉the little toe

Learning How to Write Hiragana

 Today, we're going to study hiragana.

Once you learn hiragana, you'll be able to read story books. So it'll be great fun. Let's get started, alright?

What color is this card?

 It's ao（あお）

 Good. Now, if I flip this card, there you see the characters. As you can see, this is how you write ao（あお）in hiragana.

We're going to learn how to write this first letter a（あ）of ao（あお）, okay?

Now, can you all put your index finger out, like this? Are you all ready?

First, we write across to the right, then stop.

Then, move your index finger up, and go straight down. Then, stop again.

Next, from up on the right side, you go down slowly like you are going down a tilted slope and then you make a big curve like this.

Okay, let's try again.

Did you get it?

Now, let's write the characters on the paper on your desk and practice.

 I did it!

 That looks great, Hiroshi-kun. Maybe you can practice at home too. Now, let's learn the o（お）of ao（あお）.

Point 1

letter と character の違い

letter はアルファベットや漢字、カナなど、発音できる文字を指す一方、character は文字に加えて数字や記号も含みます。英数字は alphanumeric character と言います。また、alphabet はひとつの文字体系を指します。

アルファベットの練習

 今日は、ABC のお勉強をしましょう。

この色は何色ですか？

あおいろ！

英語ではなんていうんだっけ？

ブルー！

すごいわねー。正解です。カードの裏を見ると、B、L、U、Eと書いてあるでしょ。ブルーはこうやって読むのよ。

アルファベットは26文字あります。

今日は、「BLUE」の中の文字を読み書きする練習からはじめます。「B」からはじめましょう。

はい、人差し指をだして、練習しましょう。

いいですか？では上から下にまっすぐおろして止めます。

指を最初の位置に戻して、大きな半円を2つ描きます。見てて。

カーブを描いて、もう一つカーブを描いて、はじめに描いたものの下にね。で、とめる。

はい、それではもう一度。わかりましたね。

では、みんなの机の上にある紙に練習してみましょう。

できました！

ひろし君、上手ですね。お家に帰っても練習をしてみてください。次に「BLUE」の「L」の練習をしましょう。

Learning the Alphabet

 Today, we're going to study the English alphabet.

Do you know what color is this?

It's ao（あお）!

How do you say that in English?

It's blue!

Excellent. You're right. Now, can you see the back of this card? It says B, L, U, E. This is how we read "blue".

There are 26 letters in English.

Today, we're going to start by practicing how to read and write the letters in BLUE. Let's start with B.

Put your index finger out and let's practice.

Okay, are you ready? Let's start from the top, then go straight down. Then, stop.

Put your finger back where you started, then we'll make two big half circles. Watch me.

We curve around, and then make one more curve, just below the first one. Then stop.

Let's try again. Did everyone get it?

Now, let's practice on the paper on your desk.

I'm done!

Good job, Hiroshi-kun. You can continue to practice after you go home. Now, practice the next letter in blue, L.

Point 1

日本語では、ひとつの文字でひとつの音を表し、その多くは子音と母音が結びついて成り立っています。このように、原則全ての音に母音を含む言語を syllable-timed language と言います。それに対して、英語のように子音と母音を別の音と捉え、強勢を加えて話す言語を stress-timed language と呼びます。

時計を学習しましょう

時間について学びましょう。では、こちらを見てください。これは時計ですね。

時計は、何時何分と時間を教えてくれます。

短い針さんは何時を表します。1から順に12まで数字が書いてありますね？

この数字は短い針さんのための数字で、何時を表します。長い針さんは何分を表し、60分まであります。時計をみてください。一番上に12、それからグルッと数字が書いてありますね。

数字の間にある短い線が分を表します。数字の間には5分あるということですね。長い針さんは時計の一番上の12という数字から動き出して短い線を1, 2, 3と、60まで数えていきます。さあ、数えてみましょうね。1, 2, 3・・・60ありますね。60分で1時間になります。

短い針さんは、1から12までの数で何時かを教えてくれます。短い針さんと長い針さんを見れば、何時何分かが分かるんですよ。

ひろし君は、今日何時に起きましたか？

6時です！

はい、わかりました。時計で6時はどんな風になるか、見てみましょうね。

長い針さんは0分ですから、一番上の12に動かして、短い針さんを6に合わせます。ほら、これがひろし君が起きた6時ちょうどです。

やったー！

Learning to Tell Time

 Okay, let's move on to learning how to tell time. Look at this. This is a clock.

A clock helps us to tell time by showing us each hour and minute.

The short hand shows the hours. You can see the numbers 1 through 12 on the clock, right?

These are the hours. The long hand shows the minutes, and we have a total of 60 minutes. Now, look at the clock very carefully, you see 12 on the top and you see the numbers around the clock, right?

The long hand is the minute hand and it takes 5 minutes to move from one number to the next. The little lines between the numbers are the minutes. This means you have 5 minutes between each of the numbers on the clock. The long hand, or the minute hand, starts from the 12 at the top of the clock and moves around to each line, so you count them from 1 to 60, like this, 1, 2, 3, ⋯ 60. 60 minutes make an hour.

The short hand shows the hours from the number 1 to 12. So, using the short hand and the long hand we can tell both the hour and the minutes!

What time do you wake up on school mornings, Hiroshi-kun?

 6 o'clock!

 Let's check on the clock to see what 6 o'clock looks like.

First, we move the long hand to stop at the 12, and then we move the short hand down to the number, 6. See, this is the time when Hiroshi-kun wakes up!

 Yeah!

Point 1

時間の表現

1:05 one-oh-five / five after one　　　　1:10 one ten / ten after one

1:15 one fifteen / a quarter after one　　1:30 one thirty / half after one

1:40 one forty / twenty to two

つくってみましょう ㉓ 工作編

ひらがなをアートで学ぼう
「あおむし」を作ろう

ステップ 1

今日は、ひらがなで虫や動物の名前を学びましょう。この虫を日本語でなんと言うか知っていますか？すごいわ！そう、「あおむし」です。

Let's learn some names of insects and animals in *hiragana* today! Do you know what to call this insect in Japanese? Great! 「あ (a) お (o) む (mu) し (shi)」(*aomushi*), that's it!

ステップ 2

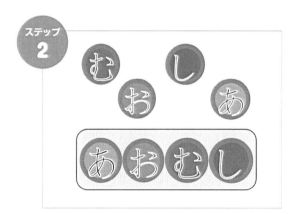

「む」「お」「し」「あ」と印刷されている4枚のカードがあります。「あ」「お」「む」「し」と正しく並び替えてみましょう。そうよ、よくできました！

There are 4 cards printed with む (mu), お (o), し (shi), and あ (a). Try to line them up in the right order: あ (a) お (o) む (mu) し (shi). Yes, you did it!

ステップ 3

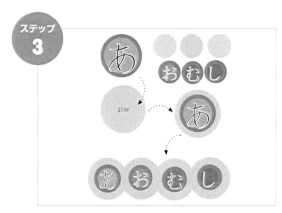

次に「あ」「お」「む」「し」のカードそれぞれを大きな丸いカードに貼りましょう。その後、、「あ」「お」「む」「し」の順番にそれぞれカードをつなげましょう。

Next, glue each of the 4 cards on to the big round cards. Then glue them together in a line, make sure your cards read *aomushi* in the right order.

Arty Hiragana - Let's Make a 'Caterpillar'

ステップ 4

ふたつの動く目、予め切っておいたモールを使って、角や足を足してください。胴体部分に糊付けしましょう。わあ！「あおむし」の出来上がり！英語では、「キャタピラー」ね。

Add some wiggle eyes and twist some pre-cut pipe cleaners for the antenna and legs. Glue them down on the body. Wow! Your *aomushi* is done. It's a caterpillar in English.

ステップ 5

では、カードに書いてある「あ」の練習をします。では、人差し指を出してください。指で「あ」を練習します。黒いお星様さまからスタートしますよ。準備はいい？
① 横にまっすぐ
② 上に上がって、下に降りてきて、ストップ。
③ 赤いお星さまに飛んで、下に降りてきて、くるっとおおきなお腹を作ってみてね。

Now, let's practice the あ (a) on the card. Show me your pointer finger. Let's practice the あ with your finger. We'll start at the black star (★). Are you ready? Let's go!
① Move your finger straight across.
② Lift it up,then down,then stop.
③ Lift it up and move it to the red star (★). Slide it down and turn your finger to make a big tummy. Okay?

ステップ 6

クレヨンを準備してください。色々な色のクレヨンを使って、練習します。虹色の「あ」を作りましょう。常に、黒い★から始めましょうね。

Get your crayon ready. We will practice this with different crayon colors. Let's make rainbow あ (A)! Remember that we always start from the black star (★)!

数字のお勉強

今日は数をどのように足すのかを学びます。はい、ここにリンゴが４個あります。では、すでにテーブルにあるリンゴに新しく３個のリンゴを足したらどうなりますか？今は全部でいくつありますか？

7個！

正解！どうやって7個だとわかったの？

最初に４個あったから、左手の指を４本立てたの。でね、３個その後足したから、右手の指を３本たてたの。それで全部の指を数えたら、7になったんだよ！

そうよ！そうするとね、こんな風に４＋３って書いて、二つのグループがあることを図にできるの。４個のリンゴに３個のリンゴを足すと全部で７個って見えるでしょ。では、逆をやったらどうなると思う？例えば、４個のリンゴがあって３個食べたら、リンゴはいくつ残っている？

1個！

すばらしい！どうやってわかりましたか？

はじめに４個あったから、左手の指を４本たてて、３個食べちゃったから３本曲げるでしょ。そしたら立ってる指が1本だから1個とわかるの。

その通りね。

４引く３はこのように書くのよ、４−３。あとね、４個のリンゴを描いて３個線で消すと残りは1個という絵も描けるわね。

Learning about Numbers

Today, we're going to learn about how to add numbers. Okay, here we have 4 apples. Now, what happens if I add 3 new apples to the apples I already have on the table? How many do I now have in total?

Seven!

Good! How did you figure out that it's 7?

There were 4 apples in the beginning, so, I put up 4 fingers on my left hand, then when you added 3 more apples, I put up 3 fingers on my right hand. Then, I counted them all together and came up with 7!

That's right. Now, I can write it out like this, 4 + 3, and make a picture to show the two groups. It looks like 4 apples plus 3 apples, which equals 7 apples. Now, what happens if we do the opposite? For example, if there are 4 apples and we eat 3, how many apples are left?

One!

Great! How did you figure that out?

You started out with 4 apples first, so I put up 4 fingers on my left hand, then we ate 3, so I bent 3 fingers down, right? After that, I only had 1 finger standing up.

Yes, you are right.

Here is how we write 4 apples minus 3, 4-3, and we can also draw a picture showing 4 apples, then cross out 3 of them, which leaves only 1 left.

Point 1

計算についての言葉

たし算	addition	引き算	subtraction
掛け算	multiplication	割り算	division
少数	decimals	小数点	decimal point
分数	fractions		

3/5　three-fifths ／ three over five

7/13　seven-thirteenths ／ seven over thirteen

図形に関する単語

二等辺三角形
isosceles triangle

直角三角形
right triangle

鈍角三角形
obtuse triangle

四角形
quadrangle
正方形
(perfect) square

平行四辺形
parallelogram

ひし形
diamond

五角形
pentagon

六角形
hexagon

円
circle

扇形
Fan shape

だ円
oval

球
sphere

円錐
cone

三角柱
trianglular prism

四角柱
quadrangular prism

円柱
cylinder

六角柱
hexagonal prism

立方体
cube

インフォメーション

検定内容・申込に関するご案内

検定日、級別レベル、出題範囲、受検方法、受検料、支払い方法など本検定に関する情報及び受検申込みについては、不定期に変更・追加となるため、本書ではご案内を掲載しておりません。
詳細については当協会幼保ホームページ https://www.youhoeigo.com でご確認ください。

幼保英語検定

教材のご紹介とご案内

本検定向けの各種学習教材は、㈱ブックフォレより出版、販売を行っております。
当協会からの直接の購入はできません。各種学習教材に関しては、
出版元の (株) ブックフォレよりご案内、ご紹介をしております。
㈱ブックフォレのホームページ https://bookfore.co.jpでご確認ください。

㈱ブックフォレ

オンライン学習ツールのご案内

単語学習につきましては、㈱mikanの専用アプリをご活用ください。

App Store: 「英単語アプリ mikan」をApp Storeで (apple.com)
Google Play: 【mikan】幼保英語検定単語帳アプリ

App Store

オンライン授業用ツール及び自宅学習用ツールとしてオンデマンド講座を開講しています。
オンデマンド講座に関する詳しい内容は、主催一般社団法人国際子育て人材支援機構(OBP) ホームページ www.obp.academyをご覧ください。

Google Play

OBP

資格カードの発行について

検定合格後、合格証以外にご希望の方には合格を証明する幼保英語士資格証を発行しています。カード形式で携帯がすることができ、身分証明書としての利用も可能です。資格証申請方法など詳しくは 幼保ホームページをご覧ください。

資格証について

幼保英語を活かした活躍について

国内及び海外での活躍の場を国際子育て人材エージェンシーでご相談を受付けております。
詳細につきましては、同社ホームページ http://www.obpjob.comをご覧ください。

OBP JOB

推薦にあたって
インターナショナルプリスクール協会(TAIP)
ごあいさつ

The Tokyo Association of International Preschools (TAIP) is a group of preschools that work together to bring professional development events and publicity to the international early childhood education community in Japan. Our organization continues to evolve with each passing year, bringing both traditional and forward-thinking methods of learning and promotion to all our members.

The organization was founded in 2005 under the motto "Preschool for Preschoolers," and now includes dozens of schools of all shapes and sizes. Many are in the greater Kanto area but others are farther away, as we continue to grow to help early childhood educators throughout Japan.

TAIP strongly supports the work of Youho Eigo Kentei as a valuable contribution to the future of Japanese education and to Japanese society at large. We will continue to back their efforts in the future.

Moving forward we will carefully consider the needs of our international members as their relevance continues to grow within the Japanese early childhood education community.

We encourage you to check our website (https://www.tokyopreschools.org/) for more information, including membership options and upcoming events.

Tokyo Association of International Preschools Board of Directors

TAIP Homepage

幼児教育・保育英語検定　準1級テキスト

2022年3月20日第二版第2刷

著　者　　一般社団法人　幼児教育・保育英語検定協会

発行所　　一般社団法人　幼児教育・保育英語検定協会
　　　　　〒153-0061　東京都目黒区中目黒3-6-2
　　　　　TEL 03-5725-3224　FAX 03-6452-4148　https://www.youhoeigo.com

発売所　　BOOKFORE　株式会社　ブックフォレ
　　　　　〒224-0003　神奈川県横浜市都筑区中川中央1-21-3-2F
　　　　　TEL 045-910-1020　FAX 045-910-1040
　　　　　http://www.bookfore.co.jp

印刷・製本　　冊子印刷社

© 2021, Organization of Test of English for Teachers　　Printed in Japan
ISBN：978-4-909846-46-4